aircraft illustrated
CIVIL AVIATION REVIEW

Edited by Leo Marriott

LONDON

IAN ALLAN LTD

£8.95

First published 1990

ISBN 0 7110 1927 4

Published by Ian Allan Ltd, Shepperton, Surrey; and printed by Ian Allan Printing Ltd at their works at Coombelands in Runnymede, England

Contents

First published in 1967, *Aircraft Illustrated* rapidly established itself as an excellent magazine for coverage of military and civil aviation in Britain and world-wide. Each issue comes full of the latest news and aircraft registration changes, articles and photo-features from many of the world's leading aviation authorities, providing a well-balanced examination of the current aviation scene.

● Edited by Allan Burney

● Published 8th of each month

● Current subscription prices available on request

Introduction

AS THIS third edition of 'Civil Aviation Review' goes to press, we stand at the start of the final decade of the 20th century — the century in which the aircraft was born and developed to perform an amazing variety of tasks. Although many of the great advances in aviation have been stimulated by military requirements in two World Wars, current and future developments are increasingly focused to the benefit of civil aviation; especially as the threat of another massive world conflict rapidly fades in the wake of the recent geo-political changes, particularly in Eastern Europe. The most rapid progress has been made since 1945 — leading to the early generation of modern jet transports in the 1960s. Since then, although the external appearance of modern aircraft has altered only in detail, there have been massive improvements in efficiency and safety through: the introduction of more powerful and reliable power units; the widescale adoption of modern electronic and computing techniques to the art of flying and navigating aeroplanes; the introduction of new materials for the construction of engines and airframes; and a myriad of design features, operating procedures, and engineering methods. In total, these have carried aviation forward to new horizons.

Many of these developments are reflected in the articles contained in this edition. An account of the world-beating Rolls-Royce RB211 engine gives an insight into the technology behind the performance of modern airliners. The practical application of the operational benefits to be accrued from the new range of fuel efficient aero engines is described in a complementary feature about the concept of Extended Range Operations (EROPS) which is now bringing the benefits of non stop intercontinental travel to an every increasing number of people around the world.

The 1990s will undoubtedly see many changes, not least in Europe where the dismantling of trade barriers in 1992 and the associated deregulation of air travel are expected to provide a massive increase in the number of passengers. How the industry will cope with this situation is yet to be determined but some signs are clear. Already major airlines are combining with, or taking over, other operators in an attempt to strengthen their positions. Lufthansa and Air France have formed a close and extremely powerful alliance while SAS has formed links with Finnair, Swissair and British Midland. British Airways and KLM have each taken a major stake in Belgium's national airline Sabena, whose history and current situation is explored in this edition.

On the manufacturing side, Europe's Aerospace industry is now in good shape with full order books and a worldwide customer base. We look at the Dutch company, Fokker, and describe the very successful Franco Italian ATR42/72 turboprop regional airliner.

Looking back over the 1980s, the outstanding European success story must be Airbus Industrie. It had sold a total of 1,331 aircraft between 1973 and the end of 1989, the lion's share of these orders occurring throughout the 1980s. In 1989 alone, no less than 583 orders and options were gained. The best seller was the new A320 and a view of this fascinating aircraft is provided in this issue of 'Civil Aviation Review'.

The traditional US airframe builders, Boeing and McDonnell, have both done well in terms of orders with Boeing selling no less than 887 aircraft during 1989 including 227 of the 757 model — illustrating the increasing popularity of twinjets for even the longest routes. McDonnell Douglas continues to sell and develop the long running MD80 series and, although plans for a propfan variant have been temporarily abandoned, the latest MD90 variants powered by the International Aero Engine V2500 are now attracting a healthy order book. The company opened the new decade with the first flight of the much heralded MD-11, an event covered in this edition.

As the face of eastern Europe undergoes massive changes, it is appropriate to look at the state of civil aviation behind the crumbling Iron Curtain. A timely article from Air Britain's Russian expert, Robert Ruffle, outlines the development of jet transports in the Soviet Union. This illustrates the fact that the USSR is now racing to catch up with western technology and may soon be producing aircraft which will sell on their own merits in a worldwide market. This will provide a new market for western engine and avionic companies and already Rolls-Royce has announced a deal to supply RB211s for the new Tu-204. On the other hand, Airbus has gained a prestigious order for at least five A310s from the state airline, Aeroflot. The face of Soviet civil aviation is undoubtedly about to change significantly over the next few years.

From the airline's point of view, the 1980s have been a period of mixed fortunes. The early years of the decade were a time of uncertainty and virtually static traffic growth — mainly associated with a world trade recession and related fuel supply and pricing problems. This in turn had led to relatively few orders being placed for new aircraft which affected all the major manufacturers. In the last half of the decade, traffic began increasing again at an average of around 6% a year, fuelling a remarkable comeback by the airlines and leading to today's bulging order books for most of the manufacturers. Whether this can be sustained over the next decade is doubtful. Many airlines are predicting a slow down in the rate of growth over the next few years. In this context the quickening pace of take-overs and amalgamations will probably lead to a number of global 'Mega Carriers' replacing the current pattern of national flag carriers on major routes.

With many airlines having placed orders for major modernisations of their fleets, many experts forecast a fall in the ordering rate of new aircraft but the increased efficiency of modern aircraft means that any airline which attempts to compete using outdated equipment will quickly fade from the scene. No doubt many famous names will disappear over the next 10 years.

Apart from airlines and airliners, this edition of 'Civil Aviation Review' also ranges across many other subjects. Philip Birtles, a long-standing contributor, looks at the history and status of Stansted Airport and reviews air cargo operations at Heathrow. In contrast, globetrotting Robbie Shaw gives us a photographic review of Canadian aviation activity. An article on Cessna's staggering range of twin-engined designs illustrates the importance of civil aviation to the business community which is relying increasingly on executive aircraft as a means of improving the efficiency of their companies. A recent report highlighted a 30% increase in orders for executive jets by British companies during 1989 in preparation for increased links with the rest of Europe.

This then is the third edition of 'Civil Aviation Review'. Airliners large and small, airlines, engines, operations, general aviation. It's all here.

FLYING THE A320

Leo Marriott

THE AIRBUS A320, despite its conventional appearance, is one of the most technologically advanced aircraft flying today. Although bearing a superficial resemblance to the current range of advanced Boeing 737s, the Airbus product has reaped the benefit of being an all new design and has been able to incorporate some startling innovations in the application of modern computer techniques to the control and operation of commercial transport aircraft. In particular, it is the first civil airliner to be equipped with a full authority computer controlled Fly By Wire control system.

Launched in March 1984, the A320 programme is proving to be another Airbus success story. The first aircraft, powered by 25,000lb-thrust CFM56-5 engines, flew on 22 February 1987 and production aircraft entered service with Air France and British Airways in April 1988. Bearing in mind the complexities of the aircraft, this was an extremely short timetable. Inevitably there were a few teething problems — mainly caused by some of the many computers overreacting to various minor deviations from standard parameters. An example of this was the aircraft's Slat and Flap Control Computer which had a tendency to lock these surfaces at a particular setting as it sensed that there was a setting error. In fact the 'errors' detected were well within acceptable limits and a simple software change cured the problem. However, the time taken to trace and rectify such problems could keep an aircraft out of service for unpredictable periods.

Happily, most of the early problems have been overcome and today the aircraft has an enviable reputation for reliability, performance and economy. This has been enthusiastically noticed by many airlines all over the world

Above:

British Airways has a fleet of 10 Airbus A320 in service or on order. These are used on a variety of European routes as well as domestic links from Heathrow to Aberdeen and Newcastle. *British Airways*

Above right:

The use of sidestick controllers in place of conventional control columns gives a spacious look to the A320 flightdeck. In front of each pilot are screens for the Primary Flight Display and a Navigation Display. In the centre are the two ECAM displays and immediately below, in the centre console, are the two MCDU displays and keyboards. *British Airways*

Right:

Capt Duncan and First Officer Bagshaw check through the weather and flight plan information produced from the FICO computerised printouts. *L. Marriott*

Below right:

Airbus A320, G-BUSH, on stand B17 at Heathrow is prepared for flight BA728 to Geneva. *L. Marriott*

GLOSSARY

AFS	Automatic Flight System
ATC	Air Traffic Control
C of G	Centre of Gravity
DME	Distance Measuring Equipment
ECAM	Electronic Centralised Aircraft Monitoring System
EFCS	Electrical Flight Control System
EGT	Exhaust gas temperature
ELAC	Elevator and Aileron Computers
ETA	Estimated time of arrival
FADEC	Full Authority Digital Engine Control System
FICO	Flight Information and Control of Operations
FMGS	Flight Management Guidance System
FMS	Flight Management System
IAS	Indicated airspeed
ILS	Instrument Landing System
MCDU	Multipurpose Control and Display Units
ND	Navigation Display
NOTAMs	Notices to Airmen
PFD	Primary Flight Display
RETARD	Autothrottle/speedcontrol mode in which throttles bleed off at programmed rate during landing fare
SEC	Spoiler and Elevator Computers
SID	Standard Instrument Departure
STARs	Standard arrival routes
TMA	Terminal manoeuvering (or control) area, ie terminal airspace
VDU	Visual Display Unit
VOR	VHF Omnidirectional radio range

who, up to the end of 1989, had ordered no less than 529 A320s with another 99 of the stretched A321 (due to enter service in 1994) also on order.

Despite the success of the whole Airbus range of aircraft, British airlines have conspicuously failed to order them in any quantity. Although a few A300s have been operated by charter carriers (Dan Air and Orion), the largest UK Airbus fleet is now flown by British Airways which currently operates 10 A320s. These aircraft were, of course, originally ordered by British Caledonian (which was one of the first A320 customers) and the order was inherited when British Airways took over BCal in 1986. In fact, the first two aircraft (G-BUSB and G-BUSC) were delivered in BCal livery and had to be hastily repainted before entering service.

Flying an aircraft such as the A320 involves a quite different approach to that required for conventional aircraft and I was therefore pleased to accept an invitation from Capt John Duncan to accompany him on a scheduled flight aboard a British Airways A320 from Heathrow to Geneva. A very experienced pilot, Capt Duncan originally flew with BCal where he was the BAC One-Eleven Fleet Manager before becoming involved in the A320 programme. Subsequently he moved to BA as a result of the take over and is now the Fleet Manager (Technical) for the airline's A320 aircraft.

I met up with Capt Duncan and his co-pilot for the day, First Officer Carl Bagshaw, in the Flight Dispatch Centre situated in Heathrow's Queen's Building. The contrast between the two pilots could hardly have been greater. Set against the experience and background of the Captain, Carl was a young pilot who had only recently qualified on the A320 after successfully passing a Commercial Pilot's training course at the British Aerospace College, Prestwick, followed by some 60 hours on the A320 simulator after joining British Airways.

Both pilots were going through the necessary paperwork before taking a crewbus out to the aircraft (G-BUSH) waiting on B17, one of the Terminal 1 parking stands. In the past this would have involved collecting sheaves of paper forms from various desks and departments in order to gather information on aircraft status and load, weather reports and forecasts, fuel requirements and costs, and navigation and routeing data. Today most of this is available at the press of a few keys from the ranks of computer terminals scattered around the room. By entering our Flight Number, BA728, into the FICO (Flight Information and Control of Operations) computer, Carl receives a printout of all data relevant to the flight. This includes relevant weather reports for airfields along the route and at the destination and alternate fields, NOTAMs (Notices to Airmen) affecting Geneva and other points, details of the passenger load as booked up to 09.30hrs that morning and various other matters. A separate printout gives a copy of the SWORD flightplan which sets out the navigation data for the route, including elapsed times and groundspeeds between various waypoints allowing for the forecast winds held in the system's memory. In addition, the fuel requirements for each sector of the flight are set out and totalled, and list of waypoint and navaid positions in Latitude and Longitude are listed so that these can be checked against the data in the aircraft's Flight Management System (FMS).

From all this information a number of salient facts are drawn and basic decisions made. The weather en route and at Geneva is unlikely to cause any problems, although a strong north-westerly jetstream is giving wind speeds of 140kt at our cruising level (FL370 — 37,000ft). Geneva is reporting a southwesterly breeze, broken cloud at 6,000 and 9,000ft, with the possibility of stronger winds and showers later in the day. The alternate airfield will be Lyons and our total fuel load, including statutory reserves, will be 5766kg. Anticipated fuel burn for the flight is 2939kg and, with over 120 passengers aboard, the take-off weight will be 60,300kg.

Our ATC departure slot, nowadays an integral feature of any commercial flight, is set at 13.30hrs so the crew complete their paperwork and are at the aircraft by 12.45hrs. This allows some 30min to carry out the routine preflight checks as the passengers begin to board from the adjacent holding lounge. Most of the checklists are contained in the aircraft's unique Electronic Centralised Aircraft Monitor System (ECAM) whose dual VDU screens occupy the centre of the pilot's instrument panel.

One of the first actions is to enter flight details into the FMS in the form of the departure, destination and alternate airfields. This is done by means of the keyboards on the Multipurpose Control and Display Units (MCDU) set into the centre console between the pilots. Also entered is the

Standard Instrument Departure (SID) to be flown and this is obtained over the radio from ATC (call-sign London Delivery) prior to start up. Today it will be a Midhurst 2F departure off Runway 27 Right. Using this information, the FMS automatically checks through the onboard database and selects the appropriate route details, including: waypoints, radio navigation aids, airways, standard arrival routes (STARs) and vertical flight profiles, and this information is then displayed automatically on the Navigation Display screen in front of each pilot. The full flight plan is also available on the MCDU screens if selected.

With all passengers on board, doors closed, and pre flight checks completed, the Captain calls for pushback and engine start at precisely 13.15hrs. Clearance is immediately forthcoming and, as the tug moves the A320 clear of away from the pier, the First Officer runs through the start up procedure for each of the two engines. This could not be simpler. Select each engine in turn and hold the start switch forward. Like everything else on this aircraft, it is entirely computer controlled. The Full Authority Digital Engine Control system (FADEC) is linked to the Electrical Flight Control System (EFCS) and the Automatic Flight System (AFS) to monitor and control the engines at all stages of the flight. During start, the computer will spool up the engine core, automatically opening the HP fuel cocks at 22% N2 and checking that the Exhaust Gas Temperature (EGT) does not go above limits. If any faults or problems are detected, the engine is automatically shut down and restarted. This will be repeated three times after which, if the engine is not functioning correctly, the computer will abort the start procedure and report engine status via the ECAM screen.

Of the two ECAM screens, the upper is normally dedicated to readout of engine parameters and warnings, while the lower is used as a system display to show the state of various ancilliary systems such as wheels, brakes hydraulics, flying controls and fuel transfers. Again, these displays are computer controlled to the extent that the pilots rarely need to access them through the MCDU. The relevant system display for the lower screen is automatically selected according to the stage of the flight. Thus prior to start, the screen will show the status of the various doors and access panels around the aircraft. Once these are all

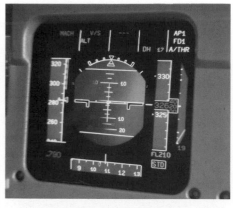

The pilot's **Primary Flight Display (PFD)** incorporates the functions of Flight Director, Artificial Horizon, Airspeed Indicator, Altimeter, Vertical Speed Indicator, Compass and Turn Coordinator. Other data including autopilot status is presented in alpha numeric form. *L. Marriott*

The **Navigation Display** in 'ARC' mode with the aircraft symbol at the bottom and the projected flight plan route shown correctly orientated. At top left are readouts showing ground and air speeds together with the current wind speed and direction while at top right is the range and bearing to the next waypoint. Other data including weather radar returns can also be superimposed on the display. *L. Marriott*

On the flightdeck as the A320 cruises over France at 37,000ft. The use of sidestick controllers allows for a convenient folding table in front of each pilot. The various EFIS displays show up clearly despite the bright ambient light. *L. Marriott*

closed and the start up procedure is commenced, the screen shows the serviceability of the wheels and under-carriage through parameters such as brake temperatures and tyre pressures, and also shows the aircraft's weight and Centre of Gravity position. As the aircraft begins to taxi, the display changes to show the settings and positions of the various flying controls, flaps and spoilers so that these can be checked and correctly set prior to take-off.

As we taxi out to the holding point for Runway 27 Right, joining a steady stream of aircraft heading the same way, there is time to take a quick look around the flightdeck which is remarkably spacious for this size of aircraft. The basic layout is fairly conventional with the two pilots sat either side of a central console containing the engine controls and selectors for the radio navigation equipment. The instrument panel is dominated by the six large VDUs while the glare shield contains the controls for Flight Management Guidance System which includes the functions of an ordinary autopilot. The two VDUs in front of each pilot are the Primary Flight Display (PFD) and the Navigation Display (ND) while the two ECAM displays are centrally located where they can be easily viewed by either pilot. Ancillary system controls are mounted in a conventional roof panel.

Behind the Captain's seat is a spare seat with a neat wardrobe for storing jackets and hats set beside it, right in the corner. On the other side is a stowed jump seat which can be slid out and positioned immediately behind the centre console to give an instructor or observer an excellent view of the whole flightdeck. The usual crew on the A320 is, of course, two pilots but it is always useful to have additional space on any flightdeck.

As our departure slot approached, we waited at the holding point and were then cleared to line up on the runway behind a landing Malev Tu154, resplendent in the airline's new livery. At precisely 13.30hrs the tower gave take-off clearance and, as the First Officer moved the power levers fully forward, the A320 began to accelerate smoothly down the runway. As power built up a characteristic rasping hum was noticeable from the big fanned engines. The Captain called out for rotation as speed passed 141kt, Gear Up was selected at 152kts and flaps were fully retracted as the speed built up

through 190kt. By this time the aircraft was passing 1,600ft and the FMGS autopilot had been selected and armed. The Midhurst 2F departure called for a complex series of turns and an accurate vertical flight profile passing fixed DME points from London at specific altitudes. Altogether the sort of flying which would tax human pilots while they coped with a busy ATC environment and would be difficult to programme into a conventional FMS.

However, on the flightdeck of the A320 there was an atmosphere of relaxed calm, even at this busy stage of the flight, as the FMGS automatically flew the SID procedue while displaying the details and the aircraft's position continuously on the ND. Two minutes after take off we were instructed to call London Control on 123.9 Mhz where the controller instructed us to maintain 6,000ft on reaching, although advising that there were no speed restrictions — normally 250kt on the London TMA. At this stage of the climb the ECAM display showed the engines functioning normally at the climb setting with a fan speed (N1) of 90%, core speed (N2) at 95.4% and an EGT of 700°C. Fuel was being consumed at the rate of around 2,600kg per hour for each engine. The instrusive engine noise which had characterised the take-off was now muted with climb power selected.

At 13.34hrs, ATC instructed us to take up a heading of 200°, followed shortly after by a turn on to 160° and clearance to continue climbing to FL130. Two minutes later, while passing through FL100 with Gatwick airport clearly visible below on the left, there came another frequency change to 127.7Mhz where clearance was given for further climb to FL290. By 13.38hrs the A320 was climbing through FL165 and had just passed abeam the Midhurst VOR. Airspeed had built up to a healthy 290kt IAS and at this point ATC cleared us direct to Mantes, a VOR just West of Paris and 149nm from Midhurst.

At 13.45hrs the aircraft was still climbing steadily at just under 2,000ft per minute as we crossed the mid channel point and were instructed to contact Paris Control on 132.82 Mhz. On making contact, clearance was given to continue climb to our cruising level, 370 (37,000ft), which was reached at 13.52hrs — only 2min later than the time forecast on the printout from the SWORD flightplan. In level flight the engines automatically adjusted to the settings needed to

maintain the optimum cruising speed of Mach 0.79 — N1 at 89%, N2 at 93.8%, EGT 660°C and Fuel Flow around 1300kg per hour. Indicated airspeed was 258kt but groundspeed was around 510kt thanks to the effect of the strong winds at this level.

Once established in the cruise, John took the opportunity to explain the aircraft's complex Fly By Wire system — the EFCS. Understandably the system is extremly complex involving multiple computers and a variety of operating modes to cover failure of any component. In simple terms there are two Elevator and Aileron Computers (ELAC) and three Spoiler and Elevator Computers (SEC — pronounced Sex!). Inputs from the pilot's sidesticks are fed through these computers which determine the control surface response to be applied. The exact response will be calculated according to various control laws, contained in the computer's software, designed to ensure that the aircraft is always flown within pre-determined parameters, which in turn depend on the stage of the flight. In normal flight, the EFCS will maintain the aircraft in a 1g situation as long as no input is received from the sidestick. In practice this means that the aircraft will maintain the last demanded trajectory, ironing out any deviations caused by turbulence, change of trim or other factors. Sidestick inputs are only required to change the actual flightpath of the aircraft. At low speeds the EFCS, in conjunction with the FADEC, will prevent the aircraft from stalling by automatically limiting the angle of attack and applying engine power. Effectively this means that the aircraft can never be flown outside its safe performance envelope, irrespective of the actions of the pilot.

The use of multiple computers provides full back up in the event of a single computer failure while the aircraft can be safely flown using only the ELAC or the SEC computers. Further redundancy is provided by using computers designed and built by different manufacturers and using different software so that a single mechanical or software fault will not be duplicated in the parallel computer. The safety implications of the EFCS are tremendous and Airbus is to be congratulated on its world-beating achievement with this aircraft.

We were now well into French airspace, following Airway UG32 approximately 120nm south of Rambouillet. A left turn at waypoint BENIB puts us on course for Autun VOR on Airway UR28, which is

crossed at 14.17hrs. With 134nm to run to Geneva, the ND indicates that it is time to begin descent and this is commenced with ATC approval. The power settings are now reduced automatically to 39% N1, 64% N2, 315'C EGT, while fuel flow is only 160kg per engine. We have a total of 2880kg of fuel remaining at this stage. Although still over France, control is now transferred to Geneva ATC as we approach SAUNI, 41nm northwest of Geneva, while passing through FL210. Another frequency change to Geneva Arrival on 131.32 Mhz leads to a series of instructions to change heading as the controller vectors us on his radar to a sweeping base leg passing a range of hills before coming on to final approach for Runway 23. As we pass through 7,000ft altitude, Autoland Mode is selected. The ILS for Runway 23 has been selected and identified automatically, and this information is shown on the ND. As we come on to final approach, we break out of the scattered cloud layer. Lake Geneva, flanked by mountains on either side, stretches out ahead. The aircraft establishes on to the ILS beams at approximately 10 miles from touchdown and speed is steadily reducing, decaying through 220kt at this point. Gear Down is selected at 175kt and the flaps are progressively deployed as indicated by the ECAM display.

Although altitude is determined with reference to sea level, Geneva airfield elevation is 1,411ft amsl and on short finals aural height warnings above runway level are generated by the radar altimeter through the FMGS. As we approach the landing threshold speed is 130kt, reducing and a deep mechanical voice intones, 'Four Hundred . . . Two Hundred . . . One Hundred . . . Fifty Feet . . . Twenty Feet . . . RETARD . . .'

The last call indicates the point at which the throttles should be closed

and the aircraft flared for landing. As this is an automatic approach the crew are interested spectators as the computers perform flawlessly and ease the A320 on to Geneva's 3,900m runway. The time is 14.36hrs only 66min since take-off from Heathrow and 3min ahead of the flightplan ETA.

Although this routine landing was made in good weather conditions, it is worth recording that the airline's A320 fleet is now certificated to land in visibilities as low as 75m with a zero feet Decision Height. These are the lowest limits of any aircraft in the British Airways fleet.

Turning off the runway, we are directed to Stand 33 alongside one of the airport's three circular satellite terminals, each with parking for up to four aircraft. As we roll to a stop by the gate, the engines are shut down and the aircraft performs its final trick. A buzzing noise at the base of the central console accompanies a computer printout of any faults or alarm indications which have been triggered by the FGMS or ECAM

during the flight. This is torn off and filed with the flight documentation — available to the ground engineers for fault rectification or systems analysis. In the near future this information will be automatically transmitted to the ground during flight so that maintenance and fault rectification will be even more efficient.

Altogether the flight has been a fascinating experience and has demonstrated that the A320 is heralding a new era in flight management, safety and operation through the use of the most up to date technology. Where Airbus has led, the other manufacturers are rushing to follow. Given this progress, one can only speculate what the new generation of pilots such as First Officer Carl Bagshaw will be flying in 20 or 30 years time. Indeed, will pilots still be needed!

In the meantime it only remains for me to record my thanks to Capt Duncan and his crew for their willing assistance in the preparation of this article.

CESSNA'S TWINS

Leo Marriott *discusses the extensive range of Cessna twin-engined aircraft, past and present*

THE WORLD'S business community was quick to see the benefits of commercial aviation and even before the outbreak of World War 2 many companies owned their own aircraft. After 1945 the concept of corporate aircraft became well established and demand for increased performance and capabilities led to the first business jets in the 1960s. Today's business aircraft are as technologically advanced as the largest airliners and many are capable of transporting executives in oppulent comfort across the major oceans or on coast-to-coast transcontinental flights in the US. The very size of the North American continent has meant that the main market for business aircraft has been centred there, but factors such as European deregulation and the staggering economic growth of Far East

countries has stimulated demand on a worldwide basis.

However, those companies which have achieved a major market share in this field are inevitably American and one of the most famous is the Cessna Aircraft Company, based at Wichita in Kansas. Founded by Clyde V. Cessna in 1927, the company's first product was the unimaginatively named Cessna Model A – a four-seater single-engined high-wing monoplane. This was the precursor of a whole range of high-winged single-engined aircraft which became something of a Cessna trademark and sold in their

thousands – production finally ending in the mid-1980s owing to falling sales and the crippling financial effect of US product liability laws. Despite this, the company remained in business by continuing to build and sell its range of successful twin-engined turboprop and jet-powered business aircraft. These aircraft, the Citation series of twinjets and the Caravan II, are the successors of an amazing range of twin-engined business and commuter aircraft built by Cessna since 1939 and forming a range unrivalled by any other manufacturer.

Below:
The Citation V is the ultimate development of this straight-winged executive jet. Distinguished externally from the Citation II by an extra cabin window, this model can cruise at 500mph and has a range of almost 2,000nm with six passengers.
Cessna

Cessna Aircraft's first twin was the Model T50, a five-seater powered by twin Jacobs radial engines, which first flew in 1939. While the type might well have been reasonably successful as a civil transport, it was subsequently built in very large numbers (4,636 delivered) as a military trainer and light transport for use during World War 2. Several found their way on to the civil market after the war and many are still flying today.

The first modern Cessna twin was the Model 310, first flown on 3 January 1953. Entirely constructed from metal, it was powered by twin 240hp Continental 0-470-B engines in tightly streamlined cowlings which gave it a maximum speed of over 220mph — faster than any other contemporary production light twin. A unique feature for the time was the fitting of streamlined wingtip tanks as standard, each one holding 41.5imp gal. The basic 310 proved itself capable of continuous development, although the most obvious change occurred with the introduction of the swept fin Model 310D in 1960, while the use of turbosupercharged engines and a rearrangement of the cabin to provide six seats resulted in the Model 320

Above:
A straight-tailed Cessna 310C photographed in 1962. This high performance twin was regarded as something of a 'hot ship' when the first examples appeared on the British register at the end of the 1950s. *Ian MacFarlane*

Below:
Cessna's first twin was the Model T-50 which first flew in 1939. Several thousand were built for military use in World War 2 and many restored examples fly in military markings today. *Ian MacFarlane*

Also derived from the basic Model 411, and eventually replacing it in production, were two more variants, the 401 and 402, which were unveiled in 1966. The main difference was the installation of lower-powered Continental turbocharged engines rated at 300hp and neither aircraft was pressurised although originally they retained the oval windows of the 411/421 range. The model 401 was intended as an executive aircraft to carry up to eight people including crew and over 400 were built before production ceased in 1973. In contrast, the 402 was intended as a cheap, rugged, commuter aircraft carrying up to nine passengers or convertible to the light freight role. Later versions, marketed as the Businessliner or Utililiner, were distinguishable by a lengthened nose and continuous row of five square cabin windows along each side. Like other Cessna models, it was also eventually built with the new wet wing with squared-off wingtips, this version being known as the Model 402C.

To add to the confusion experienced by many in identifying various Cessna models, the company produced the hybrid Model 414 (later named Chancellor) which first flew in 1968. This used the wing and lower powered engines of the 401/402 series mated to the pressurised fuselage of the 421.

Cessna's final variation on the cabin-class piston-engined twin theme was the Model 404 Titan which first flew in February 1976 and featured an entirely new airframe and wing. Powered by twin 375hp engines, the Titan could seat up to 11 passengers in the commuter role and had a maximum take-off weight of 8,300lb – making it larger and heavier than its predecessors. It could also be distinguished by a row of six square windows along each side of the cabin, a square-tipped wet wing, and dihedral on the tailplane. An executive version was known as the Ambassador while a dedicated freighter was called the Courier.

By 1984, the only Cessna piston-engined twins in production were the Models 303, 340A, 402C, 411, 414 and 421C but subsequently Cessna ceased production of these, and its single-engined range owing to falling sales and the rise in Avgas fuel prices.

However, by this time Cessna was also producing a comprehensive range of turboprop twins which continued in production to serve the corporate and airline market. The first of these to fly, in August 1976, was the Model 441 which in fact had been

Above:
Cessna's first production turboprop was the Model 441 Conquest which was developed in parallel with the piston-engined Titan. *L. Marriott*

developed in parallel with the Titan and used a pressurised version of the same airframe. Engines were 620hp Garrett TPE-331-8-401 turboprops giving the aircraft a maximum cruising speed of 337mph at 24,000ft; although it could cruise as high as 35,000ft for maximum economy in which case it could fly distances of up to 2,638 miles with reserves. Owing to the pressurised cabin, seating capacity was reduced to a maximum of 10, including the pilot, but a more common arrangement was for two crew and six passengers in a well-appointed cabin.

In 1977, Cessna began development of a turboprop version of the Golden Eagle. Known as the Model 425 Corsair, this aircraft first flew in 1978. Powered by Pratt & Whitney Canada PT6 turboprops rated at 450shp, it could cruise at just over 300mph and was normally configured for two crew and four passengers, although two additional passenger seats could be fitted if required.

With the approaching demise of the piston-engined range, some rationalisation of the turboprop range took place in 1983, mainly for marketing purposes. The Model 425 Corsair was renamed Conquest I and the larger 441, already named Conquest, became the Conquest II. All reference to Model numbers was dropped.

Over the years, Cessna had developed a profitable arrangement with Reims Aviation, allowing the French company to produce various types under licence. Thus by the mid-1980s, Reims had built more than 6,000 Cessna aircraft – mainly variants of the single-engined range including 150, 152, 172 and 177 models as well as the 337 twin. When, in 1982, the

parent company intimated that it was considering the cessation of all its piston-engined range, Reims Aviation proposed a turboprop version of the successful unpressurised Titan model. This proposal was prompted by the difficulties in the supply of Avgas, particularly in the Third World countries where aircraft such as the Titan were popular with cargo and commuter operators. The result is the Cessna 406 Caravan II which uses the basic Titan fuselage, the wing of the 441 Conquest II and the PT6A engines from the Conquest I, rated at 500shp. This combination gives an exceptional payload capacity – maximum all up weight is 9,925lb and up to 14 people can be carried.

With Cessna having now ceased production of all propeller driven twins in the United States, the Caravan II (produced only by Reimes in France) is its only product in this market. Nevertheless, with a sparkling performance and the Cessna name behind it, it should sell well for many years to come.

Back in the US, Cessna's production and marketing effort is now almost entirely devoted to its Citation range of executive jets (the only other Cessna civil production model is the single-engined Caravan I utility aircraft). Development of an executive jet began in the 1960s and the original Fanjet Model 500 first flew in 1969 powered by two Pratt & Whitney Canada JT15D-1B 2,200lb thrust turbofan engines. The basic design was kept as simple as possible and the fuselage was based on the pressurised Model 421, while a straight wing was selected to ease low speed handling problems. The turbofan engines, the first application to an executive jet, offered lower noise levels and much improved fuel consumption. A considerable number of changes were made to the basic design before the first production aircraft, now named Citation, flew in late-1971. These included a lengthening of the forward fuselage, moving the engines aft, a larger fin, and a redesigned and relocated tailplane. The Citation I could carry a crew of two and five passengers up to 1,500 miles at a crusing speed of 411mph, and it remained in production until 1985 when a total of 691 had been delivered.

The Model 550 Citation II first flew in 1977 and featured the sort of improvements which could be expected – a new high aspect wing of greater span, lengthened fuselage with seating for two crew and a maximum of 10 passengers, uprated JT15-D4 engines and increased fuel capacity. The Citation II has proved as popular as its predecessor and to date over 560 have been sold, including three to the Republic of China – the first ever sale of an executive jet to that country. The current production version is the Citation S/II which features more powerful engines and increased all up weight allowing extra fuel to be carried.

Chronologically, the next development of the basic, straight-winged Citation was the Citation V, details of which were announced in 1987 with first deliveries following in April 1989. Powered by JT15D-5A engines,

Above:
Developed from the unpressurised Titan, the Cessna 406 Caravan II is produced by Reims Aviation in France. Although unpressurised, it offers an exceptional payload for an aircraft of this category and is proving a popular workhorse. *Cessna*

Below:
The swept wing Model 650 Citation III is a very sophisticated aircraft and has little in common with its straight-winged stablemate. Its 3,000 mile range allows transcontinental coast to coast flights in the US. *Cessna*

Above right:
The new 'T' tailed Citation Jet is due to fly in 1991 and is close in size and weight to the early Citation models. Speed, range and fuel economy are all greatly improved. *Cessna*

Cessna model at the time of its entry into service.

Latest additions to the Citation range are the Models VI and VII based on the swept wing Citation III and replacing the Citation IV, development of which was announced in October 1989 but cancelled only a few months later on cost grounds. The new models will fly in 1991 and 1992 respectively.

Over the last 20 years Cessna has sold over 1,500 Citations and, since the company's formation in 1927, a total of over 177,000 aircraft of all Cessna models have been built. Although now a wholly-owned subsidiary of the General Dynamics Corporation, Cessna's unique record of meeting the needs of the business aviation community will ensure that the company's name and products will be with us for a long time to come.

the Citation features a 2ft fuselage extension to improve cabin space although seating capacity remains unchanged.

The continued increase in size, weight and performance of the Citation range resulted in a gap at the bottom of the market which had been filled by the original Citation I. Consequently, in 1989, Cessna announced the newest addition to the range – the Model 525 CitationJet. This latest design is slightly smaller and lighter than the original Citation I and carries a crew of two with four passengers. New Williams/Rolls-Royce FJ44 fanjets improve significantly speed and range while the CitationJet is visually distinguishable by its 'T' tail configuration. Like the rest of the Citation range, the new model can be certified for single pilot operation – an important cost saving feature for a corporate aircraft.

Cessna's other current production model is a swept-wing design marketed as the Citation III and IV. Although using the same name, these aircraft are a completely new design of business jet – in fact the first all new such aircraft produced in the US since the original Citation. First flown in 1979, the Model 650 Citation III is powered by 3,650lb thrust Garret TFE 731-3B-100s turbofans and features swept wings and 'T' mounted tail surfaces. Up to 13 passengers can be carried although most aircraft are supplied in executive configuration – including the first one which was sold to the golfer Arnold Palmer in 1982. With six passengers it has a range of 2,904 miles and at 22,200lb was by far the largest and most sophisticated

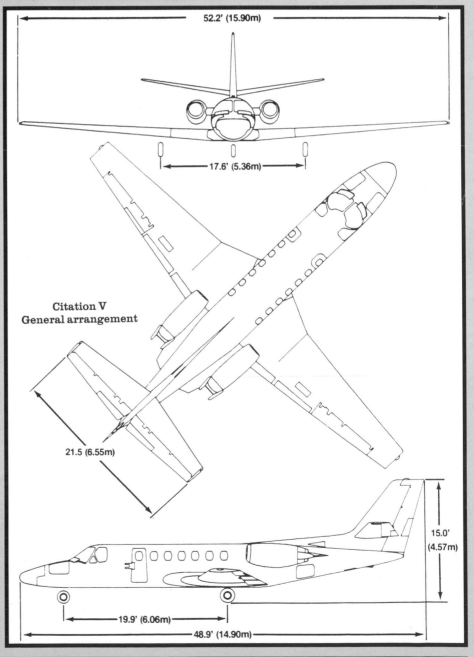

Citation V
General arrangement

52.2' (15.90m)
17.6' (5.36m)
21.5 (6.55m)
15.0' (4.57m)
19.9' (6.06m)
48.9' (14.90m)

A FEATURE of the commercial air transport scene in the 1980s has been the explosive growth of regional and commuter airlines. Across the world people are looking more and more to the aircraft as a viable means of transport, not just for long distance or international travelling but also for short domestic trips. Additionally, remote parts of the world where surface transport is impossible or inefficient have been made more accessible by aviation. Many aerospace companies saw this market forming and have produced a bewildering range of turboprop airliners to meet the need. At the smaller end of the market are aircraft in the 20-35 seat range such as the Jetstream, Shorts 330/360, Brasilia, Dash 8 and Saab

Above:
The ATR family in the air. In the foreground is the first ATR72, clearly showing the stretched fuselage and increased wingspan. With certification of the new version completed in late-1989, first customer deliveries were made at the end of the year.

340. Moving up to larger aircraft in the 40-50 seat range, the market was dominated by old stalwarts such as the Fokker F27, the British Aerospace 748 and the de Havilland Canada Dash 7 all of which were selling steadily despite the fact that the basic designs were over 20 years old.

In Europe two aerospace companies found themselves considering similar designs for twin turboprop airliners in this size category. Aerospatiale, based at Toulouse in France, had a project designated AS-35 while the

Italian company, Aeritalia was working on its AIT-230. Following an amalgamation of these design studies in 1979-81, a joint venture company named *Avions de Transport Régional* was set up in November 1981 with headquarters at Toulouse and an agreement was drawn up whereby the partners would share in the design, development and production of the new aircraft on a 50-50 basis. Reflecting the name of the new company and indicating the proposed seating capacity, the new design was given the title ATR42.

FAMILY AFFAIR
ATR Success

Leo Marriott *reviews the story behind the best-selling ATR family of turboprop airliners*

If the new aircraft was to succeed in the face of established competition, it would have to provide better performance, reliability and economies of operation than similar types — especially as there would be no first cost price advantage. For example, in 1983 the fly away cost of an ATR42 was quoted as US$6.5 million which compares closely with the US$6 million price tag on a British Aerospace 748 at that time.

In order to achieve these requirements, the design was kept as simple as possible while utilising advances in technology where this would produce positive benefits. The general layout of the aircraft was a conventional high-wing twin-turboprop, but several unusual features are incorporated. The small tailplane is set high up on the top of the swept fin and the undercarriage retracts into fuselage-mounted fairings. The latter arrangements mean that the undercarriage struts are shorter and lighter than would be the case had they been conventionally mounted in the engine nacelles, and the wing itself is lighter because it does not need to be strengthened to take the full shock of the landing loads.

Both companies had extensive knowledge of modern composite

Above:
First ATR42 customer was the French regional Air Littoral which uses the aircraft for services into London Heathrow on behalf of Air France. *L. Marriott*

Below:
Cimber Air Denmark was an early ATR42 customer, receiving its first aircraft on 20 December 1985. It currently operates three ATR 42s but a further two are flown by the airline's German subsidiary. *All photos courtesy ATR unless otherwise credited.*

materials such as Nomex, Kevlar, Carbon fibre and conventional glassfibre laminates. These are used throughout the airframe, particularly for flying control surfaces, wing leading edges, undercarriage bays, engine cowlings and the wing/fuselage fairings. The fuselage itself is an extremely simple shape with an almost circular constant cross section for the length of the passenger cabin which is faired into a straight conical tail section. The high aspect ratio wing is mounted on top of the fuselage so that the main spar does not intrude into the cabin and design of the aerofoil benefitted from the extensive computer modelling techniques already used by Aerospatiale in its Airbus work.

The selected powerplant was the Pratt & Whitney Canada PW120 turboprop driving 3.96m diameter four-bladed Hamilton Standard propellers. Each blade was moulded in fibreglass with a polyurethane foam filler, all bonded on to an aluminium alloy spar, again saving weight when compared to conventional metal blades.

For simplicity, all flying controls are operated by mechanical cable linkages, while the double slotted flaps are hydraulically operated, as is the undercarriage. The hydraulic bay is situated in the port undercarriage bay and power is provided by two electric pumps rather than the normal engine-driven pumps. This arrangement makes for simplified maintenance and inspection procedures.

On the flightdeck, ATR has introduced advanced technology on a selective basis. The primary flight instruments are glass-screen CRT based and comprise an EADI (Electronic Attitude Director Indicator) and an EHSI (Electronic Horizontal Situation Indicator). This EFIS (Electronic Flight Instrument System) is based upon twin AH600 strapdown attitude and heading reference systems, and two AZ800 digital air data computers. These, in turn, are linked to the FZ600 flight computer which controls the autopilot, fitted as standard. Also available is a Sperry Flight Management System (FMS) but this option has not been taken up by many customers. All engine and systems instrumentation is by conventional gauges and indicators. Based on its Airbus experience, ATR has gone for the 'dark cockpit' philosophy whereby no indications are received from a nor-

mally functioning system — any warning or failure light then becoming immediately apparent to the crew.

Production of the aircraft is equally shared. Aeritalia produces the fuselage, fin, tailplane and undercarriage fairings. These components are then shipped to the Toulouse final assembly line where the Aerospatiale-built wings are fitted. Flight testing of completed aircraft is also done at Toulouse.

The three year development programme called for a roll-out of the prototype ATR42 (F-WEGA) at Toulouse in July 1984 followed by a maiden flight the following month. This timetable was maintained and the milestone first flight took place on 16 August. By this time ATR already held orders and options for over 60 aircraft including launch customers Air Littoral and the American operator Command Airways.

By May 1985, three aircraft were flying in the test programmes and rival manufacturers, who had voiced

Above:
Air Pacific started operations in the Fiji islands in 1986, using two ATR42s leased from Australian Airlines. These were replaced in 1989 by two new aircraft ordered directly from ATR — one of which is shown on a test flight. The airline's longest route is a three hour overwater flight from Fiji to Western Samoa — making full use of the ATR42's long-range capabilities.

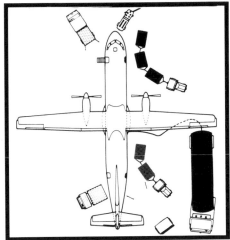

some scepticism of the performance figures quoted by ATR, waited to see if the brochure figures would be proved in the air. In fact the test programme proceeded well without any serious problems and first deliveries were made to Air Littoral's Montpelier base in December 1985.

A comparison of some basic parameters between an ATR42 and the BAe 748 provides an indication of why the Franco-Italian aircraft has done so well against its potential competitors. Despite the appelation ATR42, the basic aircraft was offered as a 46-seater with an empty weight of 21,184lb compared to 27,250lb for the 48-seater BAe 748 — a difference of around 6,000lb which illustrates the weight savings achieved by the ATR team. Although the PWAC turboprops are less powerful than the Rolls-Royce Darts on the British aircraft, the ATR42 has a maximum cruising speed of 275kt against 243kt for the 748. Economic cruising speeds are 255kt and 241kt respectively, and the

ATR42 burns only 877lb of fuel per hour at these speeds as against the other aircraft's 1,572lb per hour — a really significant saving.

With figures like these, customers were soon queueing up to buy the ATR42 and the 100th aircraft was delivered in August 1988 (to Missouri-based US regional carrier Trans World Express), less than three years after the first delivery. By the end of that year total firm orders for the type stood at 166 with a world wide customer base, although ATR must

have been particularly pleased with its penetration of the North American market which already accounted for 49 aircraft.

The base model on offer was the ATR42-200 which, since late 1988, is offered with 48 seats as standard configuration. Also available is the ATR42-300 offering improved payload/range resulting from an increased maximum take-off weight. For hot and high operations, the ATR42-320 offers the slightly more powerful PWAC121 turboprops to

Above left:
Service vehicle access around the ATR allows quick turnaround times.

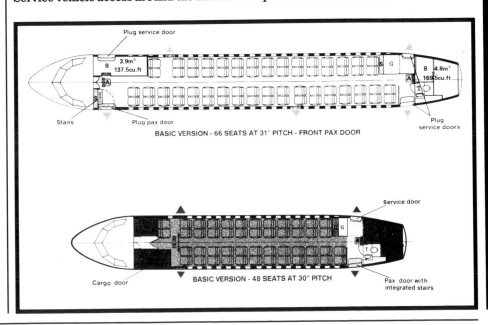

Plug service door

3.9m³
137.5cu.ft

B
A
S
Stairs
Plug pax door

G
B
4.8m³
169.5cu.ft
A
T
Plug service doors

BASIC VERSION - 66 SEATS AT 31" PITCH - FRONT PAX DOOR

Service door

G
T
O

Cargo door
BASIC VERSION - 48 SEATS AT 30" PITCH
Pax door with integrated stairs

improve take-off performance and single-engine ceiling.

Despite the success of the basic aircraft, ATR had always planned to introduce a larger model and the basic design was such as to allow production of a stretched version without too many modifications. Provisionally this was given the title ATR60, indicating the likely seating capacity of a larger aircraft, but in 1985 the project was formally announced as the ATR72 offering seating for 66 to 74 passengers — putting it into head-on competition with British Aerospace's ATP. Apart from the obvious fuselage stretches fore and aft of the wing, other changes included extended outer wing sections and redesigned engine nacelles. Power was provided by two 2,400shp (take-off rating) Pratt & Whitney Canada PW124 turboprops. Empty weight rose to 26,895lb and maximum all up weight to 44,070lb. An optional version permits operations at a maximum take-off weight of 47,400lb but as the same engines are used the sea level ISA take-off distance increases by almost 1,000ft to 5,005ft. Fly away price of the standard ATR72 was fixed at US$8.65 million.

The first ATR72 was rolled out at Toulouse early in August 1988 and, after completing ground tests, made its maiden flight on 27 October 1988. A second aircraft joined the test programme in December. First customer for the new aircraft was Finnair which ordered five, the first being delivered in July 1989. Other early buyers included the French regional TAT which ordered 20 (with 10 options), 15 of these being for its own use and the rest to be leased to other airlines. Pan Am Express is another important customer and placed an order for three (with six options) in April 1989. This was a typical repeat

Above:
In reality this aircraft belongs to Resort Air, a US commuter airline based at St Louis, Mi. With a total of seven ATR42 and 8 ATR72 in service or on order, the airline flies feeder services for TWA under the Trans World Express banner. Other TWA Express operators include Air Midwest, Henson, Jet Express, and Virgin Islands Seaplane Shuttle.

Above right:
Brit Air is one of several small airlines operating regional services on behalf of national flag carrier Air France. Although finished in the Air France colour scheme, the Brit Air name appears on the engine nacelles.

Above:
ATR made an early breakthrough into the Far East market. Taiwan-based Foshing Airlines was formed in 1988 and has ordered a total of four ATR42s. Based at Sungshan, Taipei's downtown airport, the airline flies to tourist and business centres on the island.

Right:
Karair is a subsidiary of Finnair and will use five ATR72s leased from its parent company to operate a network of domestic services. The first have been delivered this year but in the meantime Finnair already flies five ATR42s.

order from an airline which had already had a favourable experience flying the earlier ATR42 — Pan Am Express already having 11 of these in operation or on order. At the end of January 1990, orders for the ATR72 stood at 126 while the total order book for all versions of the ATR stood at 404 (including options) from no less than 44 airlines. No less than 107 aircraft were ordered in 1989 alone.

Apart from the basic airliners, ATR offers the aircraft in a number of versions for specific tasks. Most important of these is the all freight ATR42-F which has a redesigned interior, a strengthened floor and a portside rear cargo door which can be opened in flight. This version will obviously appeal to both civil and military operators and is in addition to a variant of the standard ATR42 which has a forward cargo door and a quick-change interior. Both versions can carry a 4-tonne payload in nine containers, while the quick-change version of the ATR72 can carry 11 containers.

Another specialist variant is used for the flight checking of air navi-gation aids and one of these was delivered on 14 April 1989 to ASECNA (Agency for the Security of Flight Navigation in Africa and Madaga-scar). Based in Senegal, this agency is responsible for the checking of flight aids in 15 African states including the Seychelles in the Indian Ocean. The aircraft's maximum unrefuelled range of in excess of 3,000 miles was an important factor in this order. Fur-ther developments under consider-ation include the ATR72 Advanced with more powerful PW130 engines, and a stretched 82 seater designated ATR82. A go ahead decision on both variants will be made late in 1990.

In service, the ATR42/72 family has been specifically designed for ease of operation with simple maintenance routines and good access for service vehicles on the ground. These criteria have been met and help to explain the type's popularity with many small airlines flying to remote airports with limited ground facilities. A typical example is Air Tahiti which currently operates a fleet of four ATR42s in French Polynesia. Services are flown to no less than 35 different islands in the archipelago, many of these have short rough airstrips set close to mountains. The all-pervasive salt-laden atmosphere means that engines have to be washed out with distilled water every day in order to prevent corrosion. The reliability of the air-craft in these conditions, aided by good back up from the manufacturer, has been instrumental in opening up the islands for commerce and tourism. With successful examples such as this, ATR will find no difficulty in selling its aircraft to a combination of new and established customers and in the tough world of aircraft sales it undoubtedly has a winning combi-nation.

DATA TABLE		
	ATR42-300	ATR72
Length (oa)	74ft 5in	89ft 1.5in
Span	80ft 7in	88ft 9in
Height	24ft 11in	25ft 1in
Wing area	586sq ft	657sq ft
Max take-off wt	36,815lb	44,070lb
Max landing wt	36,155lb	43,870lb
Empty wt	22,675lb	26,895lb
Max payload	9,920lb	15,765lb
Max cruise speed	265kt	286kt
Cruise ceiling	25,000ft	25,000ft

STANSTED LONDON'S THIRD AIRPORT

Philip Birtles *examines the current status of London's third airport and also reflects on its distinguished history*

THE DEVELOPMENT of Stansted as London's third airport has been a highly political and sensitive issue from its inception. Out of the controversy, the project has grown into a major civil engineering undertaking, which will make Stansted into one of the most modern airports in the world. Apart from retaining the single existing 3,648m runway, which can cope with any of today's aircraft, Stansted will be unrecognisable by the early 1990s.

At the forefront of the development is the new terminal, which will be opened in early 1991. It is a vast building, quoted to cover the area of London's Trafalgar Square. The

impression gained is that it will probably include the area of many of the Square's surrounding buildings! Despite its size, this ultra modern building is specially designed to have a low profile and, therefore, not create an eyesore in the local environment. To achieve this low profile and to maintain an effective building, a large area of ground has been scooped out to provide a hidden service area, including a dedicated railway spur from the main London to Cambridge line.

This initial phase is costing BAA (formerly the British Airports Authority) £300 million on the redevelopment of the new terminal building, plus two satellite terminals capable of handling some eight million passengers per year, as well as the development of the new airfreight terminal opened for business in mid-1989. In addition, the British Rail link (which is tunnelled under the main runway and brings passengers right into the rear of the terminal), is costing some

Below:
The newly delivered Air UK BAe 146-300, G-UKHP, flying over its main operating base at Stansted. The new terminal is under construction at top left and the new cargo centre is just above the aircraft tail.

£40 million. Particular attention is being paid to the needs of disabled people from the railway station into the terminal.

One of the satellites will be opened with the terminal in 1991, the link between the two being by a monorail system. While waiting for their aircraft, passengers will be in a lounge with a panoramic view of the airport and its operations. The second satellite will be completed soon after.

All the remaining hangars and other older buildings on the south side of the runway have been removed and replaced by a splendid new £20 million Qualitair (now FFV Aerotech), maintenance facility capable of accommodating up to two Boeing 747s. The first aircraft entered this hangar in May 1989.

The existing terminal building, on the north side of the runway, handled over one million passengers in 1988, this number having doubled over a period of three years. The capacity of 1.5 million passengers was expected to be reached during 1989, and temporary alterations had to be made to allow the terminal to maintain effectiveness for up to two million passengers a year before the new facilities are opened. The old terminal will then become a general aviation facility.

Top:
Stansted is currently home for a number of business aircraft. This usage will expand with the opening of the new terminal, as it will make the current terminal facilities available for corporate aircraft use.

Above:
McDonnell Douglas DC-8s in a variety of sizes and colours are regular users of Stansted Airport. The stretched Swiss-registered African Safari HB-IDF is one example of the charter operators.

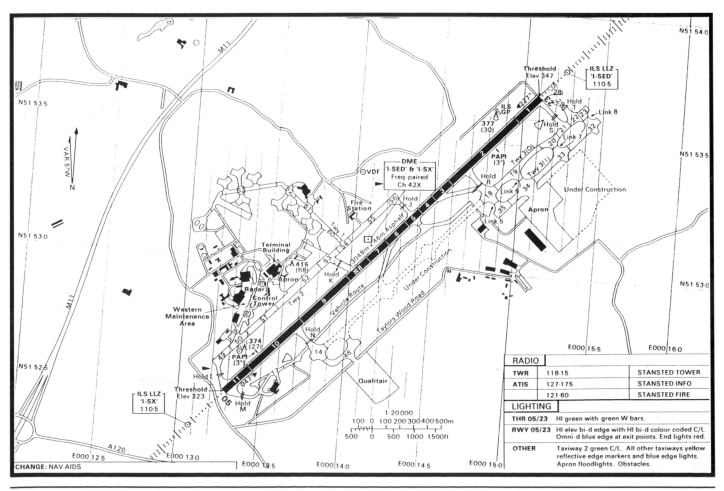

Research has shown that some 55% of Gatwick's passengers start their journey north of the Thames, making Stansted, with its easy road and rail links, an ideal point of departure or entry for a significant catchment area when full operations commence. To cope with anticipated expansion, outline planning permission already exists for Phase 2, which would handle a total of 15 million passengers per year in additional satellites. A possible Phase 3 could cope with another 10 million passengers, which would involve a further terminal building. There are no plans to build a second runway as yet, but enough land is available.

The scale of the civil engineering is vast and not just the structures themselves. Six million metres of soil have been moved around the site for landscaping. The new aprons will have an area of 666,000sq m, equal to over 60 Wembley football pitches, and the total length of the new roads is 25km. As part of the overall landscaping, 250,000 trees and shrubs are being planted.

During the development, many interesting archaeological sites have been unearthed, and with the financial help and co-operation of BAA, these have been excavated and the results preserved for future generations to enjoy.

In somewhat more recent years, the history of Stansted airfield has been varied, but nearly always as a backwater of aviation, an image which it is now rapidly losing. Construction of the original airfield began in July 1942, by the 817th US Engineering Air Battalion and the 1,919-acre airfield opened a year later as a US Forces Air Depot. By October 1943, the airfield was configured in a standard layout, consisting of a NE/SW 6,000ft long main runway and two 2,000ft runways running roughly N/S and NW/SE. The remains of these two short runways still exist although not for operations, as the old terminal is sited on one and the other is used for the parking of aircraft!

On the south side of the main runway, a maintenance area was set up to prepare Martin Marauders for combat. Stansted took on a more active role when the 344th Bomb Group B-26s arrived, beginning operations on 6 March 1944. Their initial sorties were daylight raids on targets in France, Holland and Belgium, later concentrating on bridges to foil communications in preparations for D-Day. The Bomb Group moved to France in September, leaving the

Below:
Stansted is the main operating base for Air UK and its charter subsidiary, Air UK Leisure. The latter company operates a number of Boeing 737s including this -200, G-BMOR.

Bottom:
For many years Stansted had been the dumping ground for geriatric jets of uncertain ownership. This quickly re-registered Boeing 707, with its USA registration N816JG taped on, has had engines rapidly installed for an intrepid delivery flight to another home.

Left:
The Civil Aviation Flying Unit (CAFU) has been resident at Stansted for many years. Dove G-ANUW has now been retired and is used for ground training.

Below left:
The major cargo operator based at Stansted is Heavylift with its fleet of ex-RAF Short Belfast. These aircraft are currently undergoing a major update to extend their lives into the next century. G-HLFT is receiving some minor maintenance before departing on another sortie.

Above:
Pegasus is a US charter airline which operates DC-8s to Stansted. This aircraft, N1805, is taxying for take-off from Runway 23.

Below:
A much troubled Orion Air charter, Boeing 747 N751PA, lands at Stansted for maintenance by FFV Aerotech in its new hangar.

airfield back in the support role with the 30th Air Depot Group. When the war was finished, the airfield was used as an American transit centre until handed over to the RAF on 12 August 1945 for the formation of 263 Maintenance Unit.

Civil air operations began on 14 December 1946 when London Aero Motor Services started cargo charter services with six RAF surplus Halifax VIII bombers. The company specialised in perishable goods, but the high cost of operating the Halifax and the limited cargo volume resulted in its early demise. Another operator, Kearsley Airways, began charter flights with three Dakotas and a Proctor in the summer of 1947. Meanwhile 263 MU moved out to Hitcham, Suffolk in October, retaining Stansted as a satellite base.

As a prelude to the current operations, in December 1948, the Minister of Civil Aviation considered a variety of uses for Stansted, including allocating it as the principal charter base and a major diversion airfield for the London area. In April 1949, ownership of the airfield was passed from the Air Ministry to the Ministry of Civil Aviation.

American interest was re-established in the airfield at this time,

the USAF wanting to use it for jet operations. Plans for improvement included lengthening the main runway to 10,000ft by 200ft wide, and adding 11 large aircraft hardstandings. Construction work began in February 1954 and included the building of a new parallel taxiway, which served as a runway while the main runway was being lengthened and strengthened. During this reconstruction period, over 60,000 passengers, mainly on trooping flights, staged through the airport, until work was completed in December 1956. By the middle of 1958, the USAF decided that, after all, it had no further use for the airfield unless World War 3 broke out! The site therefore reverted to solely commercial use.

The airfield then became a base for a variety of maintenance organisations and charter operators. Airwork overhauled ex-RAF F-86 Sabres for other NATO air forces and Aviation Traders acquired almost the entire ex-RAF fleet of Prentice Trainers for civilian conversion. A few emerged as five-seat tourers, and one even as a seven-seater, but the majority ended up as scrap. The last of the Avro Tudor airliners ended their days at Stansted and Skyways was amongst the charter operators.

Another resident was the Ministry of Aviation Fire Training School

Above:
The vast new diamond-shaped FFV Aerotech hangar at Stansted can hold two Jumbo jets or a combination of smaller aircraft for high quality maintenance.

Below:
Channel Airways operated a fleet of ex-BEA and Olympic Airways Comet 4Bs in the early-1970s until it became insolvent.

Bottom:
One of the later residents of the Stansted Fire School was ex-BOAC Comet 4, XA-NAP, which was leased to CMA of Mexico. It was later acquired by Channel Airways as a source of spares before ending its days on fire training.

which moved into the southeast corner of the airfield in November 1960. With it arrived a Comet 1A, Lincoln and Meteor NF14, but their 'careers' were relatively short-lived! The school has since moved to Teesside.

Meanwhile, Aviation Traders transferred its Carvair production line from Southend to Stansted in August 1961, the first 'conversion' making its maiden flight in the summer of 1962.

By the early 1960s, Stansted was a major terminal for trooping flights and also for aircrew training away from the busy runways of Heathrow and Gatwick. On the airline side, Channel Airways operated Comet 4Bs and its two Trident 1Es from Stansted, although one Trident spent most of its time as an expensive source of spares. Channel Airways eventually closed down in 1971.

In the Government White Papers of 1961 and 1964, Stansted was back in the political limelight with recommendations that it should be London's third airport, but public objection resulted in the choice of Maplin, on the mudflats beyond Southend. In 1974 this was abandoned and once again Stansted became the chosen site, which was confirmed after a further lengthy and costly public enquiry. With its closeness to the M11 and a spur link to be built, as well as the rail link, Stansted offers easy and rapid transport to London, without the hassle of Heathrow and Gatwick crowds.

On the maintenance side, Aviation Traders became Qualitair with an injection of cash from FFV Aerotech, a Swedish government-backed organisation. A vast new hangar has been constructed on the south side of the main runway to a unique diamond planform, allowing easy access for up to two Boeing 747s. FFV Aerotech is offering competitive third-party maintenance, in conjunction with another branch of the oganisation in an even larger hangar at Manchester.

Near to the Aerotech facility, is the long established Stansted resident operator, Fordair, the European Ford Company airline with a varied fleet of Gulfstream, BAC One-Eleven and BAe125. Another long-term resident of Stansted is the Civil Aviation Flying Unit which in the past has operated a fleet of Doves and BAe125s and currently use BAe748s for calibration of airfield aids.

Stansted is not only a major port for passenger operations, but also for cargo. The Short Belfasts of Heavylift are often resident and the new purpose-built Cargo Centre was opened in the summer of 1989. Currently shared by Federal Express, Servisair and Gatwick Handling, it is the classic layout of landside for road operations, and airside for aircraft with the transit shed in between. This new facility replaces the original established cargo operations using a collection of old hangars and World War 2 Nissen huts, all being cleared within the development plans.

Servisair was the first freight agent to arrive at Stansted in the early 1970s, handling build-up or breakdown of loads for all types of aircraft, from an Islander to a Boeing 747. In addition many of the regular passenger flights also carry cargo in any spare space in the cargo holds.

Air cargo provides a rapid means of transporting perishable cargo (such as fruit and vegetables, frozen foods and meat) and livestock (cattle, horses or birds etc). High value, low volume cargo is ideal for air transport, saving interest charges. Machinery is also regularly airfreighted, anything from computers to oil-well equipment, and often cars, particularly high-value classic cars for restoration and resale.

Though tonnage of airfreight at Stansted has been growing recently at a rate of about 40% per year, this is expected to level out to nearer 25%. This could well increase further if more passenger flights are attracted to Stansted, with their additional cargo capacity under the cabin floor.

The Stansted Cargo Centre offers a full transit shed capability for other ports. In effect, Stansted can accept bonded cargo in by road for export by air; in by air for customs clearance and depart by road; in by road on a bonded vehicle from another port of entry pending clearance and distribution by road; or cargo flown in and then broken down for wider distribution by air. With a minimum of eight cargo stands already operational, the future of Stansted as a transit cargo centre could expand dramatically. The cargo business is under a continual change creating highly competitive business and currently Stansted gains much of its work owing to congestion at other airports, giving it a chance in the long battle to gain acceptability.

Stansted — London's third airport — is slowly emerging from its chrysalis to become a major international gateway, transforming a World War 2 Nissen hut facility to a futuristic and environmentally acceptable airport. Stansted is now going through the growth pains similar to those experienced by Gatwick in the early 1960s. With its vast catchment area and easy surface communications, it is set to be a success for the 21st century. In terms of serving the passengers and the airlines, Stansted could easily become London's Number One airport!

Above:
Channel Airways took delivery of two out of the original five ordered, specially configured Trident 1E-140 in mid-1968. However, the airline ceased to operate in 1971 and the two aircraft were acquired by Northeast, later to be absorbed by British Airways.

MD-11 takes to the Air

THE PROTOTYPE McDonnell Douglas MD-11 trijet took off on its maiden flight from Long Beach, Ca on 10 January 1990. Piloted by John Millar, MD-11 chief of flight operations, the aircraft was airborne for 2hr 56min and carried out initial tests over the Pacific Ocean and Edwards AFB before landing at Yuma where the Douglas Aircraft Company test facilities are located. In a typical maiden flight test profile, the crew carried out a basic evaluation of the aircraft's handling, checked airborne performance against projected figures, and ran function checks on the aircraft's mechanical and avionic systems. Flight and ground test crews were also able to check and calibrate specially installed test instrumentation. In the course of this successful flight, the prototype reached a maximum altitude of 25,000ft and a speed of 300kt.

Surprisingly, the pilot in command during this important flight, John Millar, is British and an ex-RAF pilot. During his 20 years in the service, he flew Canberras and Vulcans before graduating from the Empire Test Pilot's School at Farnborough. Subsequently he was involved in various British test programmes including the TSR-2 based at Boscombe Down. In 1967 he started a three year exchange

Above:
Airborne. The MD-11 makes its maiden flight at Long Beach on 10 January 1990. Clearly visible in this unusual view are the winglets which significantly reduce drag during the cruise. *All photos courtesy McDonnell Douglas*

Below:
Pilot in command during the MD-11's successful first flight was John Miller (2nd from the right) who is an ex-RAF pilot and entered the world of test flying via the ETPS course at Farnborough.

posting at Edwards AFB where he flew a fascinating variety of aircraft including the B-52 mother ship for the X-15 and the B-58 on XB-70 chase duties. He was also the USAF project pilot on the C-5A. The opportunities for test flying in America obviously attracted John who joined McDonnell Douglas in 1970 when he retired from the RAF at the end of his US posting. Since then he has worked on a range of company projects and flew on the first flights of the DC-10-30, the KC-10 equipped with aerial refuelling pods, and the MD-87.

John's co-pilot on the maiden MD-11 flight was Tom Melody, an ex-USAF pilot with degrees in aeronautical and electrical engineering. During his USAF career he flew T-38, F-100, F-105, F-106, C-130 and WC-135 aircraft before joining McDonnell Douglas in 1986. As his specialist interests include cockpit technology, he has been closely involved in the development of EFIS (Electronic Flight Information System) systems for MD aircraft and is project pilot for the MD-88.

At Yuma, the MD-11 prototype immediately embarked on the start of a 2,000hr test programme with the objective of achieving US FAA and European JAR (Joint Airworthiness Requirements) certification in time for initial customer deliveries in November 1990. To meet this tight schedule, four aircraft will be committed to the airframe and systems test programme while a fifth will carry out a 400hr certification programme for the Pratt & Whitney

Top:
The MD-11 production line at Long Beach showing the first three aircraft in the final assembly bay. By 1993 a complete aircraft will roll of this line every six days.

Above:
A pair of winglets frame this head on view of the first MD-11 on the production line. Apart from these surfaces, other aerodynamic improvements on the aircraft include a redesigned wing trailing edge, a smaller horizontal tail to reduce drag and an extended tailcone.

Below:
Stop — Aircraft Crossing Ahead! The first MD-11 is towed from the final assembly shed to the flight test line across a public highway, Lakewood Boulevard.

PW4460 engine which is offered as an alternative to the General Electric CF6-80C2 installed in the baseline aircraft. Two of the first four aircraft will be allocated to checking out the new digital avionics system which includes a two crew EFIS cockpit.

To speed service entry, the MD-11 will initially be certificated to derivative aircraft standards but eventually it will meet all requirements for new aircraft including new amendments which give greater safety margins in the event of an engine failure on take-off.

Although the first flight took place some nine months behind schedule, it was nevertheless an important event for McDonnell Douglas which, with the run down of DC-10 production, has lacked a long-range high-capacity aircraft to offer in competition with Boeing and Airbus products. The MD-11 project was formally launched in December 1986 with 12 initial customers including Federal Express which is due to take delivery of the first production aircraft in November 1990. Production began in March 1988 and current plans call for a rate of five aircraft every four weeks by 1993.

Currently, the MD-11 is on offer in three distinct versions. The baseline MD-11 has a fuselage 5.64m longer than the DC-10-30 from which it is developed and can seat up to 405 passengers in an all economy layout. Maximum take-off weight is 273,289kg (602,500lb) including a maximum payload of 55,566kg (122,500lb), almost 10 tonnes more than the earlier DC-10-30. Range with maximum payload is 6,000st miles but with full tanks and a reduced load (293 pax plus baggage) range increases to 8,230st miles. These figures represent improvements of over 25% compared to the DC-10-30 at comparable seating capacities. All this is achieved at no increase in the rate of fuel consumption, a tribute to the improvements in engine technology.

An all-freight version, designated the MD-11F, has a maximum payload of 93,304kg (205,700lb) carried on main and lower deck cargo holds with a total capacity of over 600 cu m. External dimensions are identical with the baseline variant and range with maximum payload is 4,076st miles.

The other version on offer is the MD-11 Combi with an aft main deck cargo bay capable of taking up to six 96in by 125in pallets while the reduced main passenger cabin can seat up to 214 in a two class

configuration. The lower cargo door is increased in size and an automated cargo handling system is installed in the lower holds where up to 32 standard LD3 containers can be stowed. Maximum payload of this version is 68,447kg (150,900lb).

All three versions are currently available with either the CF6-80C2 or PW4000 series engines, but the Rolls-Royce Trent is available for aircraft delivered from 1993 onwards. Launch customer for the Rolls-powered version is the British operator Air Europe which ordered six aircraft (with a further 12 options) in February 1989.

These will be engined by the RB211-524L Trent engines offering 65,000lb thrust with a growth potential to 80,000lb. Air Europe originally became the 17th customer for the MD-11 when it announced in December 1988 that it would be leasing three aircraft from the Japanese Mitsui leasing company pending the delivery of its own aircraft in early 1993.

Another potential UK operator will be British Airways which inherited an order for three MD-11s with six options when it took over British Caledonian. The initial plan was to take delivery of the aircraft with the

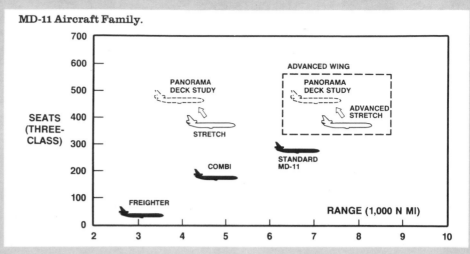

MD-11 Aircraft Family.

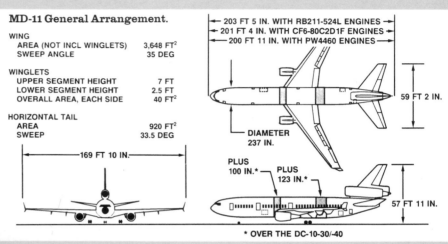

MD-11 General Arrangement.

WING
AREA (NOT INCL WINGLETS) 3,648 FT²
SWEEP ANGLE 35 DEG

WINGLETS
UPPER SEGMENT HEIGHT 7 FT
LOWER SEGMENT HEIGHT 2.5 FT
OVERALL AREA, EACH SIDE 40 FT²

HORIZONTAL TAIL
AREA 920 FT²
SWEEP 33.5 DEG

169 FT 10 IN.

203 FT 5 IN. WITH RB211-524L ENGINES
201 FT 4 IN. WITH CF6-80C2D1F ENGINES
200 FT 11 IN. WITH PW4460 ENGINES

59 FT 2 IN.

DIAMETER 237 IN.

PLUS 100 IN.* PLUS 123 IN.*

57 FT 11 IN.

* OVER THE DC-10-30/-40

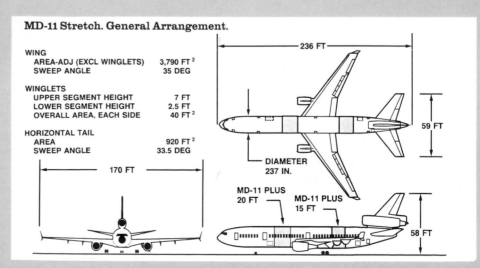

MD-11 Stretch. General Arrangement.

WING
AREA-ADJ (EXCL WINGLETS) 3,790 FT²
SWEEP ANGLE 35 DEG

WINGLETS
UPPER SEGMENT HEIGHT 7 FT
LOWER SEGMENT HEIGHT 2.5 FT
OVERALL AREA, EACH SIDE 40 FT²

HORIZONTAL TAIL
AREA 920 FT²
SWEEP ANGLE 33.5 DEG

170 FT

236 FT

59 FT

DIAMETER 237 IN.

MD-11 PLUS 20 FT   MD-11 PLUS 15 FT

58 FT

Above:
An artist's impression of the MD-11F in the colours of launch customer, Federal Express who will take delivery of the first aircraft in November 1990.

intention of leasing them to other airlines. To this end, a joint leasing company was formed with GPA (Guiness Peat Associates) which had ordered two aircraft with two options. The combined fleet of 13 aircraft will be delivered from the end of 1990 to 1993 and current favourable BA experience with the DC-10s taken over from BCal give rise to the possibility that the MD-11 may yet fly in BA colours as a TriStar replacement. However, strong competition may be expected from the Airbus A330/340. Apart from an increase in size over the DC-10, the MD-11 offers a number of other substantial changes and improvements. These include a two man 'glass' cockpit with EFIS, a revised wing with winglets for improved cruise performance, a smaller tailplane, relaxed stability and new engines. The use of advanced technology avionics is crucial to the MD-11 programme. As well as using now standard EFIS and Flight Management Systems (FMS), the requirement for a third pilot or a flight engineer has been eliminated by the use of computerised Automatic Systems Controllers (ASC) which are contained in the overhead panels where they can be viewed or reached by either pilot. The ASC checks and operates all aircraft hydraulic, electrical, environmental and fuel systems by means of independent duplex computers for each of the four systems. Engine operation is via the Flight Control Computer which, as well as performing autopilot and flight director functions, also interfaces with the Full Authority Digital Electronic Control (FADEC) engine system. Using this system, engine power settings are continually monitored and adjusted to meet the requirements of the stage of flight and pilot demands.

Although the MD-11 is only just on the threshold of entering service,

McDonnell Douglas is already looking at a further development known as the MD-11 Stretch. As the title implies, this version incorporates a fuselage stretch of 10.7m (35ft) which will allow a total of 520 passengers to be carried in an all economy configuration. One other modification which could be incorporated in this variant is the conversion of some of the lower cargo hold to a passenger seating area holding up to 99 economy class seats and taking possible passenger capacity to a total of 619 — although most airlines would obviously operate in a mixed-class configuration which would bring a typical capacity to around 450-500 seats. Nevertheless, this capability puts the MD-11 firmly into competition with the well established Boeing 747 while offering the economies of three engines. A feature of the lower deck passenger area is the fact that, owing to the fuselage cross section at this point, the cabin windows would be angled downwards giving an excellent unobstructed view of the ground. For this reason, McDonnell Douglas have termed the concept the 'Panorama Deck'.

A further development of the MD-11 Stretch will incorporate a redesigned and repositioned advanced wing but, because of the development costs, the company is looking for a risk sharing partner. Whether it will be successful in this remains to be seen. Airbus would have been an obvious partner but such an aircraft would be a direct competitor with developed versions of the A330/340.

However, the basic MD-11 is now picking up a steady stream of orders and appears to have a bright future ahead. In the opening weeks of 1990, several significant orders were announced including 20 aircraft for

Singapore Airlines and 15 for the major European carrier, KLM. In mid-February 1990, total orders and options stood at 340 aircraft — an excellent figure when it is considered that the total number of DC-10s built was only 446.

The MD-11 has started the 1990s in style but will face fierce competition from other aircraft which are due to fly in the next few years. These include the Airbus A340 and A330 which will fly in 1991 and 1992 respectively while the recently announced Boeing 777 twinjet project may well fly before the end of the decade. McDonnell Douglas will be working flat out for the rest of this year to get the MD-11 certificated and into service so that it can fully consolidate its commanding lead.

MD-11 TECHNICAL DATA		
Wingspan	169ft 6in	(51.7m)
Length oa	200ft 10in	(61.2m)
Height oa	57ft 9in	(17.6m)
Wing area (inc Aileron)	3,648sq ft	(339sq m)
Sweepback	35°	
Landing Gear		
Main Wheel Track	34ft 8in	(10.6m)
Wheelbase (fore and aft)	80ft 9in	(24.6m)
Standard Weights		
Ramp Wt	605,500lb	(274,650kg)
Max T/O Wt	602,500lb	(273,289kg)
Max Land Wt	430,000lb	(195,045kg)
Fuel Capacity	38,650 USgal	(146,290lt)
	258,966lb	(117,465kg)
Performance		
Max Payload	122,500lb	(55,566kg)
Max Level Flt Speed	588mph (945km/hr), M.87 at 31,000ft	
Take Off Field Length	9,970ft (3,040m), MTOW ISA+15	
Range with Reserves	8,039st miles, 323 pax + bags	

Fokker - Holland's high flyer

Leo Marriott *looks at the history of this famous Dutch aerospace company, from the Spider of 1910 to its new-generation Fokker 100 and Fokker 50 airliners*

DESPITE BEING one of Europe's smallest countries, the Netherlands has always been in the forefront of civil aviation development. The national airline, KLM, was one of the great trail blazers between the wars and today is a major international carrier with a worldwide network of services. In the design and construction of aircraft, the Dutch aircraft industry is today synonymous with Fokker Aircraft — a company with 13,000 employees working at six sites throughout the Netherlands and builder of the highly successful Fokker 50 and Fokker 100 airliners. In an era when most major aerospace projects are the result of international programmes, the Dutch company has

retained its corporate identity and the design leadership for its products, while still bearing the name of the man who founded the enterprise in the years before WW1 — Anthony Fokker.

Born on Java in 1890, Fokker and his parents returned to Haarlem, near Amsterdam, during 1894. Although he showed an aptitude for things mechanical, his school career was otherwise undistinguished. In 1910 he persuaded his parents to pay for him to attend an automobile engineering school at Bingen in Germany, but

he was disappointed with the standard of training available and moved on to another school at Zahlbach. This also offered training in the construction and flying of aircraft.

Here Fokker was involved in the design and construction of a prototype aircraft which eventually failed to fly. However, his appetite for aviation was thoroughly wetted and he went on to share in the construction of a further aircraft which crashed on its first flight. In typically confident style, Fokker decided that he could produce

Below:
A Fokker 50 destined for Malaysia Airlines on a test flight over the Dutch coast. Note the slim engine nacelles housing the Pratt & Whitney Canada PW125B turboprops and the upturned wingtips. The airline has nine aircraft on order.
All photos Fokker BV unless otherwise credited

a better design on his own and, together with a partner who provided some cash and an engine, went ahead and produced his first aircraft. Called the *Spin* (Spider), this was a simple monoplane with a bird-like tail and no rudder. With Fokker at the controls it first flew at the end of 1910, although his partner wrecked the aircraft in a crash shortly afterwards. From this accident-strewn beginning, Fokker went on to build several variants of the basic Spider design and by the outbreak of war in 1914, he had an aircraft factory and flying school at Scherwin and another flying school at Johannistal near Berlin. He had already sold a few aircraft to the German Army and much of his flying school business came from potential military pilots.

Whilst the Spider and its derivatives served a purpose, they were not suitable for operational military use and in 1914 Fokker was so impressed with the qualities of the contemporary Morane Saulnier monoplanes, that he obtained an example by rather devious means. Subsequently, in conjunction with his designer Martin Kreutzer, he produced a much improved version which was designated the Fokker M5. This aircraft was developed in many versions — the most famous being the Fokker E1 (Einedekker) which was the first aircraft to mount a fully synchronised machine gun firing straight ahead through the propeller. It was on this aircraft that German aces such as Immelmann and Boelcke gained many of their earlier victories and the type was referred to as the 'Fokker Scourge' in the popular press of the day.

Although the E1 was outclassed by later developments, Fokker leapt ahead again in 1916 with the highly manoeuvrable Dr1 Triplane made famous by von Richthofen — Germany's highest scoring ace of WW1. The Dr1 was designed by Reinhold Platz, a gifted practical engineer who had taken over from Kreutzer and was to continue as Fokker's chief designer until 1931. Platz was also responsible for the Fokker DVII which entered service in 1918 and was assessed by the allies as the best German fighter of the war. Although a conventional biplane in appearance, its great technical advance was the use of fully cantilevered wing structures which required no wire bracing, although interplane struts were fitted to reduce wing flexing.

At the end of the Great War, Fokker was a very rich man, having made a

Top:
The FII was the Fokker company's first commercial aircraft to be built after the end of World War 1. Powered by a 185hp BMWIIIA engine, it carried four passengers in the enclosed cabin and was one of the world's first really practical air transports.

Above:
Developed from the single engined FVIIA, the three-engined FVIIA-3m first flew in 1925 and several were used for long distance pioneering flights. Lt-Cdr R. Byrd USN used the prototype in 1926 to make the first flight over the North Pole and in 1928 Charles Kingsford Smith became the first pilot to cross the Pacific from America to Australia in his Fokker tri motor named *Southern Cross*.

Above:
Several variants of Fokker designs were built in America during the 1920s and 1930s. This example is a 14-seat Fokker F10A known as the Super Trimotor and was developed from the earlier 12-seat F10. The basic design was sturdy and reliable but the crash of a TWA F10 during a thunderstorm in 1931 led to an unwarranted loss of confidence in Fokker machines and the eventual end of American production.

fortune from his massive military contracts. But the signing of the armistice put all this in jeopardy, especially as the allies had specified that all Fokker DVII aircraft should be handed over or destroyed. However, Fokker was a most resourceful man and succeeded in dispersing and hiding much of the machinery and materials from his German factories and in a spectacular smuggling operation involving six railway trains, he was able to move hundreds of aircraft, engines and spare parts into Holland.

Here, assisted and encouraged by the Dutch government, he set up a new factory and continued to produce military aircraft for a wide range of customers including the US, Russia, Romania and the Dutch services. Initially Platz was left behind at the Schwerin factory where he started work on a series of civilian aircraft as the company was now prohibited from involvement in military aircraft production in Germany. The first design was designated the FI but this was abandoned in favour of the more sophisticated FII which featured a high mounted thick aerofoil cantilever wing and carried four passengers in a fully enclosed cabin behind the open two seater cockpit. This aircraft was the start of the famous range of Fokker civil aircraft and was used by KLM and *Deutsche Lufthansa* as well as numerous small airlines.

The next design was the FIII, first flown in 1921, which seated five passengers in the cabin while the pilot sat in an open cockpit beside the engine! Despite this odd arrangement, the design was quite popular and it was built both at Schwerin and at Fokker's new Amsterdam factory, while others were produced under licence in Germany by Grulich at its Staaken factory.

In 1921, Platz finally moved to Holland, and in this year produced the Fokker FIV. This followed the successful high wing and enclosed cabin layout of the earlier designs but could carry 10 passengers. Only two were built and both were eventually sold to the US Army.

The aircraft which really established Fokker as a major producer of civil airliners was the Fokker FVII, first flown in 1924. This was originally a single-engined high-wing cabin monoplane carrying 10 passengers and was designed by W. Rethel in the traditional Fokker layout. By this time Fokker was living in America promoting the sale of his aircraft. When he heard of an aircraft reliability trial organised by the industrialist Henry Ford in 1925, he immediately instructed Platz to redesign the FVII to be powered by three 200hp Wright Whirlwind engines instead of the single 400hp Jupiter radial engine. The resultant aircraft, the FVIIA-3m, won the trial in convincing style and led to major orders from American and European airlines. To meet the demand a factory was set up in America which produced several Fokker designs until a fatal crash involving a TWA Fokker F10 tri-motor in 1931 led to loss of confidence and closure of the production line.

The basic three-engined design was continually developed throughout the late-1920s and early-1930s, culminating in the Fokker FXVIII — five of which were built in 1932 and used for long-range flights from Holland to the Dutch East Indies. By the mid-1930s, the Fokker tri-motors with their thick wooden wings and fabric covered steel tubed fuselages, were becoming outclassed by the modern designs using all metal construction and more streamlined shapes. In an attempt to match these developments, the Fokker FXX was produced. Although still a tri-motor, it featured a retractable undercarriage, closely cowled radial engines and a much cleaner airframe.

Above:
The Fokker FXVIII was the last of the traditional Fokker tri motors. In 1933 this example, PH-AIS, made an epic 6,400 mile flight from Amsterdam to Curaçao in the Dutch West Indies in a time of 55hr and 58min carrying 100kg of mail — the first direct air link to the West Indies.

Below:
The largest Fokker airliner built between the wars was the FXXXVI which first flew in 1934. Originally intended for long range flights with 16 passengers in sleeping cabins, it was only used on European routes with a conventional 32-seat cabin layout. In this view, a Fokker DXVII fighter is parked under the port wing.

However, it was no match for the contemporary DC-2 and DC-3 and only one example was built.

Fokker's biggest airliner prior to the outbreak of WW2 was the FXXXVI, a four-engined high wing transport carrying up to 36 passengers on short European routes. However, even this was outclassed by the current American designs and Fokker cleverly hedged his bets by obtaining the European agency for the sale of the Douglas machines with an option to produce these aircraft under licence.

The war clouds were now gathering and the Fokker company was in the forefront of the development of military aircraft. In particular, the twin boom Fokker G1 twin-engined fighter, first flown in 1937, was a potential world beater and attracted many export orders, although few were completed by the outbreak of war in 1939. The Fokker aircraft to see most action in the early period of hostilities was the dated, but sturdy and effective, DXXI single-engined fighter with a fixed undercarriage. A total of 36 were delivered to the Dutch Air Force and no less than 93 were built under licence in Finland.

The outbreak of war meant the end of the old Fokker Company in more

Above:
In front-line service with the Dutch Air Force at the outbreak of World War 2, the Fokker G1 was a revolutionary twin-boom design capable of further development. Although they performed well in action, their numbers were insufficient to halt the advancing Germans. However, the aircraft illustrates well the advanced capability of the Fokker company at that time.

ways than one. Sadly the founder, Anthony Fokker, died in New York on 23 December 1939 at the age of only 49. In May 1940, German forces invaded Holland and took over the factories which were later used for the production and repair of various German aircraft, including the Bu181B Bestmann, Arado 196 float-planes and Dornier 24 flying boats. However, the workforce did its best to delay and undermine this effort. Furthermore, in 1943 severe damage was done to the Amsterdam factory by allied bombing. The Germans evacuated the facilities during September 1944, stripping them bare in the process, and by the end of the war the Dutch aircraft industry had virtually ceased to exist.

Fortunately one of Fokkers' directors, van Tijen, had managed to move three million Dutch Guilders of the company's capital to the security of a New York bank just before the war and this money was available to get the factories started again. Machinery was gradually recovered (in one case from a barge full of lathes which had been deliberately sunk in the River Amstel when the Germans invaded) and orders for gliders and the refurbishment of ex-military DC-3s got things moving. In 1946 the Dutch government provided another DFL two million to keep work going on new types including the Fokker S11 primary trainer and an amazing range of imaginative projects including a twin-jet airliner — the F26. Subsequently the production lines were kept busy with the licence-production of various aircraft includ-

ing Sea Furies and Meteors while in later years these were followed by Hunters and Starfighters — mostly for the Dutch and Belgian armed services. Today this tradition continues as the company produces licence-built F-16s.

While all of this work was welcome and helped to put the company back on its feet, the Fokker name was still absent from the civil air transport world. In 1952, an order was received for the licence-production of six SAAB Scandia airliners, but already a home-grown design was being developed. Originally designated P275, this aircraft was envisaged as a twin-engined

high-winged 32-seater and was loosely based on work carried out for the prewar F24 design which was of similar size and layout. However, in a bold and far sighted step, the Fokker management decided from the outset that the aircraft would be powered by the new turboprop engines which offered the promise of greater power, less weight and vibration-free flight. Market research in Canada and the US confirmed the basic soundness of the concept, but there was considerable resistance in the early stages to the use of turboprops. By 1952, the design had grown to a fully pressurised 36-seater and the Rolls-Royce Dart was selected as the powerplant. In this guise it became the F27 — later named the Friendship — and the first proto-type flew in November 1955. By this time, experience with the British Viscount airliner had created a favourable attitude to turboprops and Fokker received several orders from major airlines as well as reaching an agreement with Fairchild for licence-production in the US. It is interesting to note that the rival British Handley Page Herald, almost identical in size and concept to the Friendship, lost out heavily in the sales battle owing to the fact that it was originally designed around piston engines and only belat-edly re-engined with Dart turboprops.

First production F27s were delivered in 1958 (to West Coast Airlines and Aer Lingus) but this milestone was accompanied by a disastrous slump in orders which put the future of the programme in doubt for two years. However, sales picked

Below:
The Fokker company's return to building commercial transports after the war started with licence production of six SAAB Scania 40-seater airliners for the Brasilian airline VASP in 1952.

Top:
Fokker really hit the big time with its successful F27 Friendship. The prototype, shown here, first flew in 1955 and apart from a slight lengthening of the fuselage to increase seating capacity, the basic design continued in production for 30 years.

Above:
Air Wisconsin took delivery of the 786th and last Friendship in 1987 bringing its F27 fleet up to a total of 14 aircraft.

Above:
A total of 241 F28 Fellowships were sold around the world. Korean Air's order for four Mk 4000 versions was a signficant breakthrough for Fokker in the important Pacific Rim market.

up again and the rest is history — a total of 786 Friendships having been produced when production ceased in 1987. The final civil variant was the Series 600 which was powered by 2,140shp Dart RDa7 Mk 532-7R engines, could seat up to 56 passengers in a high density configuration, and featured a large cargo door as standard.

Despite the success of the F27, the company was already beginning to consider a jet-powered successor as early as 1960, although it was 1964 before the project was formally launched under the designation F28 Fellowship. This aircraft was a joint project with MBB of Germany and Shorts of the UK, which were risk-bearing partners, the latter being responsible for the building of the wing sets. The F28 first flew in 1967 and was, by today's standards, a conventional design with twin tail mounted Rolls-Royce Spey turbojets, a slightly swept wing, T-tail and a rather chubby fuselage seating up to 65 passengers in a five-abreast layout. A unique feature was the clamshell airbrake at the aft end of the fuselage. Orders totalled a respectable 241 when production ceased in 1987, although this was not as many as Fokker had hoped for initially. The F28 was produced in four versions, culminating in the F28 Mk 4000 which could seat up to 85 passengers in a fuselage stretched to 82ft 3in. Only two examples of the Mk 6000 with increased span and slatted wings were built.

Although both the F27 and F28 were selling well, by the beginning of the 1980s the company was again looking to the future, particularly in respect of a possible successor to the F28. Initially, some work was done on a new project (tentatively designated the F29) which resembled a stretched F28 fuselage with twin wing mounted turbofans. This project was soon abandoned in favour of a much larger aircraft to be developed in conjunction with McDonnell Douglas under the designation MDF-100. This short-lived scheme was terminated in 1982 leaving Fokker to revert to looking at improving the basic F28.

There was strong interest from airlines in a jet-powered 100-seater and it was decided that a re-engined F28 could meet this requirement. Work went ahead under the designation P332 on a project powered by two of the 12,500lb-thrust Rolls-Royce Tay engines which were then under development. A further increase in fuselage length to 92ft 1in

Above:
This artist's impression of the projected F29 shows a family resemblance to the Fellowship although the large turbofan engines are wing mounted.

allowed seating for up to 107 passengers and maximum all-up-weight rose to 98,500lb. Launched in 1983 as the Fokker 100, the new aircraft flew for the first time in November 1986 by which time it had secured orders for eight aircraft from launch customer Swissair, another 10 (with five options) from KLM and, most significantly, for 20 plus 20 options from the American major, US Air. The development programme was delayed by the need to incorporate a substantial number of improvements and modifications requested by major customers, but the Fokker 100 gained Dutch RLD certification in November 1987 and the US FAA followed suit in May 1989.

First customer deliveries were made at the end of 1988.

The Fokker 100 was originally intended as a low cost derivative of the F28 and it was expected that around 80% of the earlier aircraft's airframe and systems would be common to the Fokker 100. In fact this proportion has been reversed and apart from an external similarity, the Fokker 100 only shares a less than 20% commonality with the F28. A major improvement is the incorporation of a modern 'all-glass' flightdeck with a 'dark cockpit' philosophy. Collins EFIS and Automatic Flight Control System are fitted as standard allowing the aircraft to carry out Category IIIA autolandings — a unique capability to this size of aircraft.

Despite early setbacks, the Fokker 100 is now riding on the crest of a wave and by February 1990 orders and options had been placed for a total of 382 aircraft including a massive order for 75 aircraft (plus another 75 on option) from American Airlines.

Back in 1980, when serious effort was being directed to an F28 successor, it was thought that the popular F27 was nearing the end of its production life, but a resurgence of

Below:
Swissair was the launch customer for the Fokker 100 and worked closely with the manufacturer in finalising the aircraft's specification. The airline has now taken delivery of all 10 aircraft ordered.

Above:
An order for 20 Fokker 100 aircraft plus 20 options from US Air in 1985 was a major breakthrough into the lucrative American market. Fokker had to invent a special method of polishing the completed fuselages in order to produce the mirror-like natural metal finish demanded by the airline.

first flew in December 1985 with first customer delivery, to the German airline DLT, in August 1987. The aircraft has sold steadily and looks set to continue the success of the original F27 with 135 orders and options from 16 airlines placed by February 1990.

The simultaneous development of two brand new aircraft, coupled with flagging sales of the older types, created a major cash flow problem for Fokker and this resulted in a significant financial structuring of the company and a considerable cash injection by the Dutch government. However, the success of the Fokker 100 and Fokker 50 now means that this will pay off in the future. Already Fokker is erecting a new assembly hall at its Schipol plant in order to cope with a projected production rate of 67 aircraft a year for the Fokker 100 and 34 Fokker 50s per year. By European standards these are substantial numbers and will be achieved in 1993.

In addition to these projects, Fokker also builds parts for other aircraft including the Airbus A300 and A310, and also wings and struts for the Shorts 360. On the military side, production of the F-16 is projected to continue until 1992 although attrition orders may bring further orders — and on the horizon is the possibility of the European Combat Aircraft.

Were he alive today, Anthony Fokker could gaze with satisfaction on a company which is a true worldbeater in its field and which over the years has proudly borne his name to every quarter of the globe.

interest in turboprops from expanding regional airlines led to consideration of a successor under the designation P335. This project eventually became the Fokker 50, officially announced in 1983 coincidentally with the launch of the jet powered Fokker 100.

Like its stablemate, improvements over the original F27 centred mainly on the provision of a new powerplant. The Rolls-Royce Dart had given sterling service but was basically 1940's technology, whereas the new Pratt & Whitney Canada PW125B turboprops offered all the benefits of current trends — lower weight, more power, better fuel consumption. In addition six-bladed Dowty Rotol propellers significantly reduced noise levels while a completely redesigned interior greatly enhanced comfort for up to 58 passengers (standard layout is for 50 seats). Obvious external changes included a row of more but smaller cabin windows and small upturned wingtips. The Fokker 50

Below:
Production facilities at Fokker's Schipol plant are already at full stretch to meet demand. Additional capacity will become available in 1992 when a new assembly hall is completed and production will increase to 67 aircraft per year in 1993.

SABENA

BELGIUM'S WORLD AIRLINE

Leo Marriott *reports on British Airway's newest partner in the run up to European deregulation*

THE GATHERING PACE of European unity, spurred on by recent trends in the democratisation of Eastern Europe, is providing great opportunities for the continent's airlines to expand their activities across national borders without restriction. The major beneficiaries of this will undoubtedly be the largest carriers offering extensive feeder services to major hubs connecting with long-range international services. Airlines such as British Airways, Lufthansa, Air France and SAS will all be battling for a major share of the inter-European business, supported in many cases by networks of commuter services flown by small, subsidiary operators. How-

ever, this situation will be difficult for some of the medium-sized airlines which will have to fight hard to retain their existing share in the marketplace while avoiding a total take-over by their larger rivals.

An airline which clearly falls into this category is Belgium's national airline – Sabena. As one of the Benelux countries sandwiched between France and Germany, and only a few sea miles from the UK, Belgium has

always been a major crossroads for European transport systems – even before the age of the aeroplane. Today Brussels National Airport, Sabena's base, is a vital hub which is being hungrily eyed by other major users including KLM and British Airways.

Sabena (*Societe Anonyme Belge d'Exploitation de la Navigation Aerienne*) was officially formed in 1923 as a government-owned successor to two smaller companies which had started

Below:
The airline is currently upgrading its 737 fleet with the purchase of the latest CFM-56- powered variants. Shown on the ground at Brussels are four of Sabena's six 737-300s while four -400s and 12 -500s are also on order for delivery in 1991/92.
Sabena

Top:
During the early-1960s, this Bristol Freighter Mk 32 was leased by Sabena for cross channel freight operations between Southend, Antwerp and Brussels.
Ian MacFarlane

Above:
A long serving Sabena DC-6 on the apron at Heathrow in 1964. The Belgian airline was the first European operator of the DC-6 and took delivery of its first aircraft in 1947. *Ian MacFarlane*

Further commercial development was abruptly terminated when the German Army over-ran Belgium in May 1940, although the airline remained active in the Belgian Congo throughout the war, almost entirely in support of the allied war effort. By 1945 it had a route network covering 20,000 miles throughout Africa flown by a fleet of Lockheed 14 Super Electras and Model 18 Lodestars.

In Europe, Sabena restarted operations in 1946 from the ex-military airfield at Zaventem near Brussels using Douglas DC-3s for its European network and DC-4s for the long distance flights to the Belgian Congo. In addition, a transatlantic service to New York, routeing via Shannon and Gander, was inaugurated in 1947. A hallmark of Sabena's postwar operations has been its determination to offer a good quality service using the most modern aircraft available. Thus it was one of the first European airlines to take delivery of the new Convair CV-240, adding the improved CV-440 to the fleet in 1956. For the long range routes, Sabena was the first European airline to operate the Douglas DC-6 which offered substantial performance and payload improvements over the DC-4. The last piston-engined aircraft to be ordered

operations in 1919. These were SNETA (*Societe National pour l'Etude de Transports Aeriens*) and LARA (*Ligne Aerienne du Roi Albert*), the former having flown various European services from Brussels while the latter pioneered aerial communications in the Belgian Congo. When Sabena was formed, it took over SNETA's routes and in the years that followed expanded its European network to serve most of the major capitals.

More dramatically it built on LARA's experience and eventually, in 1935, started a regular fortnightly service from Brussels to Leopoldville using the ubiquitous Fokker FVII-3M — later replaced by the three-engined Savoia Marchetti S73 seating up to 18 passengers. Other aircraft flown by Sabena in its early days included the Handley Page W8b and W8c, de Havilland DH50 and Westland Wessex. Just before the outbreak of war in 1939, the airline was operating a small number of Ju52/3ms and four SM83s while, like many of its contemporaries, it had also taken delivery of the famous DC-3 which was doing so much to revolutionise air transport at that time.

Above:
The Boeing 737 replaced the Caravelle and Boeing 727 in Sabena's fleet from 1974 onwards. This example is one of 11 Boeing 737-200s while another four Series 200C were also ordered with uprated JT8D-15A engines and higher operating weights.
Sabena

was the DC-7C, the first of eight being delivered in 1957.

In the meantime, Sabena was pioneering an entirely new field of civil air transport operations when it started experimental mail services in August 1950 using Bell 47D helicopters. Subsequently, a regular postal service between Brussels and Maastricht in Holland was set up using Sikorsky S-55 helicopters. This was the first ever international mail service by helicopter and the experience gained was put to good use when the airline started passenger-carrying helicopter services. Initially using the S-55s, but later standardising on a fleet of six S-58s, an extensive network linking Brussels with 11 other cities, including Paris, was built up. Unfortunately, the operation of helicopters, even today, is extremely expensive compared to conventional aircraft and the airline's brave pioneering effort was finally abandoned in 1966 for economic reasons.

Sabena entered the jet age in 1960 when its first Boeing 707-329 began services to New York on 23 January, followed a few days later by an inaugural jet service to the Congo. The latter service was short lived as, with the granting of the independence to the former Belgian colony, the route was handed over to Air Congo (later renamed Air Zaire) on 28 January 1961, although Sabena continued to provide technical assistance.

For its European services, the airline ordered the Sud Ouest SE210 Caravelle and the first of these started operations in January 1961 on the Brussels to Nice route. A total of 10

Above:
OO-SGA was the first of two Boeing 747-100 delivered to Sabena in 1970. They are currently being replaced, after 20 years service, by two 747-300 Combi with a stretched upper deck and facilities for carrying a mixed passenger and cargo payload. *Sabena*

Below:
One of Sabena's five DC-10 Srs 30CF. This aircraft's range and payload characteristics were ideally suited to the airline's network of long-range routes and, like the 747s, can be configured for a mixed payload. The DC-10s are due to be replaced by Airbus A340s in 1993/94. *Sabena*

Caravelles was ordered and these were supplemented in 1967 by an order for six Boeing 727 tri-jets. Both types were eventually supplemented and replaced by the Boeing 737, the first of 11 737-229s entering service in 1974. All the 727s and all but one Caravelle had been withdrawn by 1977 allowing the airline to standardise on the 737 for its short and medium-range routes.

During all this time, the airline built up its base at Zaventem, now renamed Brussels National Airport, and the growing passenger traffic led to a major development of the airport's facilities commencing in 1956. A new modern terminal, incorporating ATC and technical services, was opened in 1961 but was almost destroyed in a catastrophic fire the following year. It was subsequently rebuilt and in 1973, a satellite terminal was opened on the south side of the main building to give additional aircraft gateways.

Like all the major international airlines, Sabena was quick to join the wide-bodied revolution once these air-

craft had entered service and the first of two Boeing 747-129 (OO-SGA and OO-SGB) was delivered in November 1970. However, the airline's long-range routes, which by this time included several Middle and Far East destinations as well as the established African and North American services, were judged to be better served in most cases by a smaller aircraft and consequently the first of five McDonnell Douglas DC-10-30CF was received in September 1973.

In the 1980s, Sabena has continued its policy of maintaining a modern fleet, investing in a range of the latest fuel-efficient airliners. By now there was a total of 15 Boeing 737-200s in service but, in 1985, orders were announced for six of the new -300 model with CFM-56 engines and the last of these was delivered to Brussels in 1989. Additionally, two 747-300 with the stretched upper deck were ordered for delivery in 1989 and 1990 to replace the elderly -100 series aircraft. However, the biggest order in recent times, announced in June 1988, was for four Boeing 737-400 and 12 737-500 aircraft and these will eventually replace the older 737 models in the fleet when deliveries commence in mid-1991. This order meant that Sabena will be one of the first airlines in the world to operate every version of the best selling Boeing 737. To support this investment, the airline purchased a 737 simulator which is suitable for training crews on the -300, -400 and -500 variants and this came into operation at the end of 1989.

Above:
Sabena has operated three A310s since 1983. This example (OO-SCC) is the sole A310-300, the other two being shorter ranged series -200 aircraft. *Sabena*

Apart from its commitment to Boeing products in recent years, the airline also became an Airbus customer in 1983 when it took delivery of the first of three Airbus A310-200/300. Although few in number, these aircraft have obviously made a good impression with Sabena which has become one of the launch customers for the four-engined A340. This long-range aircraft is ideally suited to the airline's network, which

Above:
Sobelair is Sabena's charter subsidiary and two of its aircraft are shown together with a Sabena Boeing 737-300 on the tarmac outside the Sabena Technics maintenance facility at Brussels. This organisation is now the only European overhaul centre for the older Boeing 707 which explains the presence of the Zaire-registered example in the background. *Sabena*

includes a number of 'long thin' routes, and when delivered in 1993/94 will replace the long serving DC-10s.

Thus by the early 1990s, the airline's fleet will consist entirely of modern state of the art aircraft — A340s and 747-300s for the long-range sectors and the three A310 and a fleet of advanced 737s for the rest of the network. The airline's balanced and steady approach to ordering aircraft will certainly have paid off.

Like many other major airlines, Sabena is a parent company to many other concerns and one of these is its charter subsidiary, Sobelair. This was formed as far back as 1946 to operate charter flights to the Congo where it also flew a number of internal services from 1957. The Congo operations were terminated in 1962 following independence but this fortunately coincided with the start of the package holiday boom in Europe and this market is now Sobelair's main activity. Its current fleet consists of a single Boeing 707-300Q (OO-SBU), three Boeing 737-200 and one 737-300. Two of the 737-400s on order for parent Sabena will be allocated to the subsidiary.

Today it is fashionable for major carriers to own or co-operate with small regional airlines to provide feeder services and to assist in the development of new routes. Sabena is no exception and currently owns a 49% stake in Antwerp-based Delta Air Transport (DAT) which is also partly owned by KLM, the Dutch carrier having a 33% stake. Formed in 1966, DAT was originally a subsidiary of the *Compagnie Maritime Belges* and it currently operates a fleet of two F28 jets, three Fairchild-built FH227 Friendships, seven Embraer EMB120 Brasilias and newly-delivered BAe 146s. Services flown by DAT are fully integrated into the Sabena time-table and the F28s supplement the 737s on a variety of shorter range European routes while the Friendships and Brasilias are used on various commuter routes and to develop regional services.

Although not a subsidiary, Sabena has entered into a marketing agreement with London City Airways to promote services between Brussels and London's Docklands airport using the latter company's Dash 7 aircraft. Currently there are four flights a day in each direction — those originating from Brussels bearing Sabena flight numbers.

In addition to its airline activities, Sabena also operates the Belgian national flying school on behalf of the government. The school's fleet of single-engined SIAI Marchetti SF260 and twin turboprop Embraer EMB121 Xingu trainers are painted in the airline's blue and white colour scheme.

To support this extensive fleet, the airline's engine and airframe maintenance is carried by a further subsidiary — Sabena Technics — which has extensive hangars and workshops at

Below:
DAT is partly owned by Sabena and provides a network of regional services using a fleet of F28s, FH227 Friendships and Brasilias. The fleet will be supplemented by eight BAe 146 currently on order. *Sabena*

Brussels National. This company was set up in 1987 by separating its functions from that of the parent airline. The new arrangement allows for closer monitoring of engineering costs and also gives the opportunity to bid for work outside the airline and thus make more efficient use of the sophisticated facilities available. Thus Sabena Technics carries out overhauls on a variety of aero engines for many customers including Air Inter, KLM, Transavia and the Belgian Air Force.

Sabena also has holdings in a number of companies engaged in aviation-related activities and several of these are wholly owned and subsidiaries. These companies include: aircraft leasing, catering services, duty free goods and shops, refuelling services at Brussels National, hotel chains and travel agencies. Altogether

the Sabena group of companies employ approximately 10,000 staff of which some 1,500 are aircrew, including cabin staff.

Despite Sabena's own efforts to modernise its fleet and react to market demands, its future is closely bound to developments over which it has little control. The most immediate of these is the continued development of Brussels National airport to meet anticipated passenger traffic in the 1990s and beyond. In this respect, the airline feels that the efforts of the Belgian Terminal Company (BATC), which is responsible for improving and expanding the terminal facilities, is not keeping pace with demand and a lack of gates will artificially restrict the airline's growth.

The deregulation foreseen after 1992, will create a commercial

environment different from that on which the airline had based its traffic forecasts when ordering new equipment a few years ago. Already SAS has made approaches, proposing an integration of intercontinental routes but this was turned down. Many airlines, particularly KLM and British Airways looked at Sabena and Brussels as a way of increasing their own market share and breaking out of the congestion at London's airports. Indeed, both airlines announced in 1989 that they would each be taking a small shareholding in the Belgian airline (around 5%). However, British Airways halted discussions on this when it became involved in the massive, but unsuccessful, takeover bid of the US major United Airlines. With that move apparently blocked, the British airline again held talks with the Sabena management which resulted in both British Airways and KLM each taking a 20% share in the Belgian airline. Each airline gained two seats on the board of directors and the reconstituted company was subtly renamed Sabena World Airlines. For an investment of $54 million, British Airways has gained an important foothold in mainland Europe and will promote Brussels as a major hub for both regional and intercontinental services.

Sabena already has ties with other airlines through the GALILEO Computer Reservation System (CRS). The battle between the various CRSs to sign up more airlines to their systems has been well documented. Basically there are two American systems, SABRE and APOLLO run by American Airlines and United respectively, and two rival European systems, AMADEUS and GALILEO. Of these, AMADEUS is used and jointly run by Lufthansa, Air France, SAS and Iberia while its rival includes British Airways, KLM, Swissair, Alitalia and others as well as Sabena. It can be seen that the Belgian airline is already being drawn closer to KLM and BA.

For the moment, Sabena retains its national independence but in the post-1992 environment it is questionable whether a medium-sized carrier such as this can survive on its own. Almost certainly it will become involved in closer commercial links with the other carriers and the day may come when it will be only an operating division of a major pan European airline. In the meantime it continues to fly, as the wording on the side of its aircraft proudly proclaims, as a World Airline.

Above:
One of DAT's seven Embraer EMB-120 Brasilias photographed during a turnround at Brussels. These pressurised high performance turboprops offer a high level of comfort for commuters to the EEC capital. *Sabena*

Below:
A Boeing 737-300 undergoes a post delivery check inside Sabena Technics main hangar. *Sabena*

SOVIET JETLINERS

Robert J. Ruffle *of the Russian Aviation Research Group (Air Britain) provides an insight into Aeroflot's jet transports*

THE WORLD'S largest airline, Aeroflot — Soviet airlines, is an integral part of the Soviet economy through its responsibility for all civilian aircraft operations. Not only for domestic and international airline and cargo services, but for all agricultural work, aerial survey, fishery protection, ice and forest fire patrols and aeromedical services.

Little known and rarely photographed, the very first jet type operated by Aeroflot was the Ilyushin Il-20, a demilitarised Il-28 bomber. A small number were employed from 1955 as express transports with one of the prime roles being to ferry newspaper matrices for *Pravda* and *Izvestiya* editions published in Sverdlovsk, Novosibirsk and other distant cities. In addition, it was employed to a lesser extent to familiarise crews and ground facilities with jet operations pending introduction of the jet airliner.

'Russia's Secret Plane' proclaimed the London newspaper headlines following the surprise arrival at London Airport of the Tupolev Tu-104 prototype on 22 March 1956. Introduction of the Tu-104 on domestic routes on 15 September 1956 ushered Aeroflot into the jet age and thus marked a milestone in Soviet civil aviation. Just prior to his death in 1953, Stalin authorised Tupolev to proceed with construction of a jet airliner, a decision that had a far reaching effect on Aeroflot services and the entire supporting infrastructures. Echelons of technicians, aircrew and airport staff had to be trained in new techniques in order to effect the smooth integration of the Tu-104. So dramatic was its introduction that over 80 airfields had to be up-graded immediately, with many more following.

Trans-Union flights by Il-12 or Il-14 piston-engined airliners taking up to 18hr with seven to nine technical stops, were slashed overnight to 5½hr

with only one stop. Powered by two AM-3 turbojets rated at 14,880lb each and developed from the Tu-16 bomber (NATO codename 'Badger') with minimum structural and component changes, the Tu-104 proved a most reliable aircraft and gave Aeroflot almost 25 years of continuous service. It entered service in 1956 as a 50-seater and progressed to accommodate 115 passengers through variants Tu-104A, Tu-104B, Tu-104D and Tu-104V. As a tribute to its service with Aeroflot, the first line aircraft is preserved on a Pedestal of Glory facing the terminal building at Moscow's Vnukovo airport. Comparable in size to the DH Comet, the Tu-104 had a range of 2,650km and Aeroflot operated some 190 of all variants. A feature of all Tupolev designs up to the late-1960s was the glazed nose which proved its worth for dead-reckoning visual checks in

remote parts of the Soviet Union during the early years of jet operation where navigation aids, even if serviceable, were sparse. The first international service by Aeroflot jet was made by a Tu-104 to Prague on 12 October 1956. As the scope for more and more international routes improved with better political relations, the Tu-104 was the first to introduce the Aeroflot emblem to the Asian and African continents. During the first 10 years of service the Tu-104 carried over 28 million passengers and no less than 80 million by its withdrawal from service in 1981.

Smaller brother of the Tu-104, the Tu-124, was evolved to meet a specification issued in 1957 calling for a modern transport to replace the Il-14 on routes shorter than 1,800km. Although from a distance almost indistinguishable from the Tu-104, the Tu-124 was a completely new

Below:
The rarely photographed Il-20, a demilitarised Il-28 bomber, provided Aeroflot with its first experience of jet operations and was mainly used for high-speed mail flights. *R. Ruffle Archives*

design. Powered by two D-20P turbofans, it entered service on 2 October 1962 on the Moscow-Tallin route, becoming the world's first turbofan short-haul transport. The main service variant was the Tu-124V seating 56 passengers and total production was about 100 aircraft, including those operated on behalf of the armed forces. It remained in Aeroflot service until the mid-1970s and proved another popular and reliable type.

Mainstay of the current Aeroflot jet airliner fleet are some 100 Il-86 wide-bodies, 250 Il-62s, 700 Tu-154s, 100 Yak-42s, 500 Tu-134s and around 400 Yak-40s. Only a fraction of this vast jet fleet is utilised at any given time, but those so designated, in conjunction with turboprop types, serve about 3,600 stations within the Soviet Union and 96 countries on the international network.

Most recent of these, the Ilyushin Il-86, is still in the final phase of series production. It entered service on 26 December 1980 on the important Moscow-Tashkent route and first flew international services during mid-1981. This is now the front-line aircraft of the long-range fleet. However, the Il-86 is reportedly not meeting the designed payload-range performance and consideration is being given to replacing its NK-86 turbofans with a later engine. Four low-bypass Kuznetsov NK-86 turbofans are mounted below wings 707-style and the Il-86 is approximately the same size, weight and power of the DC-10 Srs10. This 350-seater features powered stairways (for passengers with carry-on baggage and coats) to the lower deck for use at airfields with limited handling facilities.

The basic Ilyushin Il-62 joined Aeroflot on 10 March 1967 and

Top:
The Tupolev Tu-104 was Russia's first true jet airliner. The prototype flew in 1955, commercial operations began in September 1956, and the type was produced in several versions including the 100-seater Tu-104B shown here. *R. Ruffle Archives*

Above:
Although similar in outline to the Tu-104, the later Tu-124 was much smaller with seating for a maximum of 60 passengers. Intended for short-range routes, it was the first jet airliner to be powered by turbofan engines. *R. Ruffle Archives*

Below:
Although it first flew in 1963, the four-engined Il-62 is believed to have remained in production until 1988 with approximately 240 delivered. The Il-62s configuration inevitably led to comparison with the contemporary Vickers VC-10 and, indeed, the performance and dimensions were remarkably similar. *R. Ruffle Archives*

Above:
The massive Il-86 is typical of the more modern Russian aircraft which closely follow western design practice. Approximately 100 of this 350-seater aircraft are believed to have been ordered but payload/range performance is reported to be disappointing and a new variant with Soloviev PS90A engines will enter service this year.
L. Marriott

because of its striking similarity was frequently dubbed the VC-10ski. A good long-range aircraft, it was the first large intercontinental jet airliner built in the USSR — with seating for 168 in normal configuration and powered by four Kuznetsov NK-8-4 turbofans. Progressively improved through the Il-62M and Il-62MK, both using Soloviev D-30KU engines with clamshell reversers and greater range, it operated on international routes for 20 years and is now probably one of the better known Soviet airliners. This model is also operated on behalf of the Soviet government for VIP flights and a number of aircraft are fitted-out with special communications equipment.

By far the most prolific everyday airliner on Aeroflot's network is the Tupolev Tu-154, in its A, B, B-1, B-2 and M variants. Seating up to 180 passengers, this workhorse of the Soviet skies has also proved a most reliable aircraft — slightly larger than the Boeing 727-200 but with a vastly superior rate-of-climb, cruising speed and operating ceiling. First delivered to Aeroflot in August 1970, it is destined to remain in service at least until the mid-1990s. Engines are three Kuznetsov NK-8-2 or NK-8-2U with the improved Soloviev D-30KP fitted on the Tu-154M offering more economic performance.

The Yakovlev Yak-42 originally entered service in 1980 but was withdrawn in 1982 for technical reasons, not returning to Aeroflot until late-1984. It is now established on a network operating out of Moscow/Bykovo, with about 100 in total service. The very protracted development period thwarted the original plan for this type to become the standard regional transport with a planned production of 2,000 to replace, not only the Tu-134s which as a result remained in production

longer than expected, but other various types including some An-2 biplanes. The Yak 42 is an attractive aeroplane with a well appointed cabin seating 120, similar in size to the Boeing 727. Three Lotarev D-36 high-bypass ratio turbofans provide power, mounted as on the American aircraft. Its present production status remains unclear, but rumours of a stretched 140-seat Yak-42M persist.

On the shorter routes, Aeroflot employs large numbers of Tupolev Tu-134s, with most now brought up to Tu-134A-3 standard as a result of progressive improvements since the first aircraft entered service in September 1967. Roughly comparable to the DC-9 in size, the Tu-134 seats between 64 and 84 depending on the variant, although all are powered by

Below:
Shown on display at Moscow's Park of Industrial and Economic Achievements in 1989, the Yak-42 trijet has not been a success and the type was withdrawn from Aeroflot service between 1982-84 to allow unspecified problems to be rectified.
R. Ruffle

Top:
The Tu-154 is widely flown by the state airlines of several communist bloc countries, as illustrated by this Balkan (Bulgarian Airlines) Tu-154B used for holiday charter flights from the UK. *L. Marriott*

Above:
Developed from the Tu-124, the Tu-134 features rear-mounted engines and the final variants could seat up to 96 passengers. Around 600 were produced and it is still widely used by several east European airlines including this example flown by Interflug, the German Democratic Republic state airline.

the Soloviev D-30 series of turbofans. In addition to domestic routes, it is often seen operating international services and charter flights. Again, this is another Tupolev design offering very reliable service and may be expected to remain in operation until the mid-1990s. Production was extended beyond that originally envis-aged, when the Yak-42 failed to meet the planned programme.

Yakovlev Yak-40s are found throughout the Soviet Union servicing all the smaller locations the larger types are unable to reach. Very rugged, this STOL performance tri-jet has been an unmitigated success story. It has replaced all piston-engined airliners, plus some An-2 biplanes on short-haul routes since entering service with Aeroflot on 30 September 1968. Seating between 24 and 32, it is powered by three Ivchyenko AI-25s. About 900 Yak-40s have been delivered and although many of the earlier deliveries have now been withdrawn from use, several hundred remain active.

The last day in December 1968 saw a milestone not only in Soviet aviation, but in world terms, when the Tupolev Tu-144 lifted into the air for a 30min test flight, thus becoming the first SST (Supersonic Transport) in the world to fly. The financial, industrial and political intrigue surrounding the development of this striking SST could fill a book. Suffice to say the

aircraft presented to Aeroflot in December 1975 for initial route proving trials was a totally redesigned aircraft from that which first lifted from a snow covered aerodrome seven years earlier. During the extensive trials period, Mach 1 was first exceeded on 5 June 1969 and Mach 2 on 26 May 1970 and it is known later to have reached Mach 2.4. In its construction, the Tu-144 made extensive use of titanium alloy. Production models had a wing span of 28.80m and fuselage length 65.70m, both greater than the first prototype. Power was provided by four afterburning Kuznetsov NK-144 turbofans rated at just over 44,000lb each. It is debatable as to whether Aeroflot really took delivery of the Tu-144 in the accepted sense and it is probable that all Aeroflot operations, if not with Tupolev or Ministry of Aviation Industry personnel physically aboard, would have been closely

monitored by these organisations. Route proving flights, initially with cargo – a frequent Aeroflot practice with new types – began on the Moscow-Alma Ata line on 26 December 1975, covering the 3,260km sector in just under a block time of 2hr. (This aircraft, CCCP-77106, is now displayed at the Soviet Air Force Museum at Monino.) Starting 27 February 1977, a series of 50 proving flights began on the Moscow-Khabarovsk

route. The Aeroflot aircraft seated 140 passengers, 11 in first-class forward cabin, 30 in mid cabin and 99 in rear cabin. About five years later than planned, scheduled flights on the Moscow-Alma Ata service started on 1 November 1977, although five of the next six flights were cancelled for technical reasons. Over 100 revenue flights had been completed before the Tu-144 was suddenly withdrawn from service on 1 June 1978, following a

Below:
Despite high expectations and a prolonged development programme, the supersonic Tu-144 was a commercial failure and at least two aircraft were lost in accidents — including a tragic mid-air break up at the 1975 Paris Air Show. *R. Ruffle Archives*

fatal accident to another Tu-144 which was not in airline service. At this point it is believed 10 production aircraft had been completed. Just over a year later, on 23 June 1979, we hear of the SST again, this time as the Tu-144D flying from Moscow to Khabarovsk, a distance of 6,185km in 3hr 21min. This variant was reportedly 50% more economical in operation and apparently powered by engines, designed by the Koliesov Bureau, which also met international noise emission standards. Little or no activity followed and in August 1984 Head of Aeroflot's international traffic division Nikolai Poluyanchikh, announced the carrier had decided, after years of tests and a few months service, that the running costs of the Tu-144 were too high to justify its use.

With the 14.2% reduction in military spending announced in 1989, the Sukhoi Design Bureau, a prime military contractor, is already turning its sights towards the civil market with an ambitious programme. Chief designer Mikhail Simonov is talking to Gulfstream, Dassault and Piper on joint-venture projects, some of which will undoubtedly contribute to his envisaged Aeroflot 'second generation' SST by the year 2000. This will be larger and carry significantly more passengers than the ill-fated Tu-144. He said in August 1989 that his bureau is working on three SST projects with initial test flights expected 'within two years' and forecasts that the era of subsonic passenger aircraft is limited to 20 years! By this time he envisages Aeroflot to be operating only SSTs on route sectors of over 3hr (subsonic presumably?). His first SST will be the Gulfstream joint-venture business jet, with plans in hand for an SST fuelled by liquified methane and propane and another by liquefied hydrogen. The engineering and technical problems must be considerable, but given the product quality supplied to the military, we may expect to look forward to some interesting aircraft ranking the name of Sukhoi with those already familiar in the civil field. Simonov says in respect of SST operations with Aeroflot 'It should be a normal transport aircraft for people beyond the year 2000 and accessible by them'.

Less demanding future transports which may be expected to form the Aeroflot jet fleet of the 1990s include the Tu-204, Il-96 and possibly the Tu-334 or Yak-42M.

An aesthetically pleasing design, the Tupolev Tu-204 may be compared with the Boeing 757. It completed its

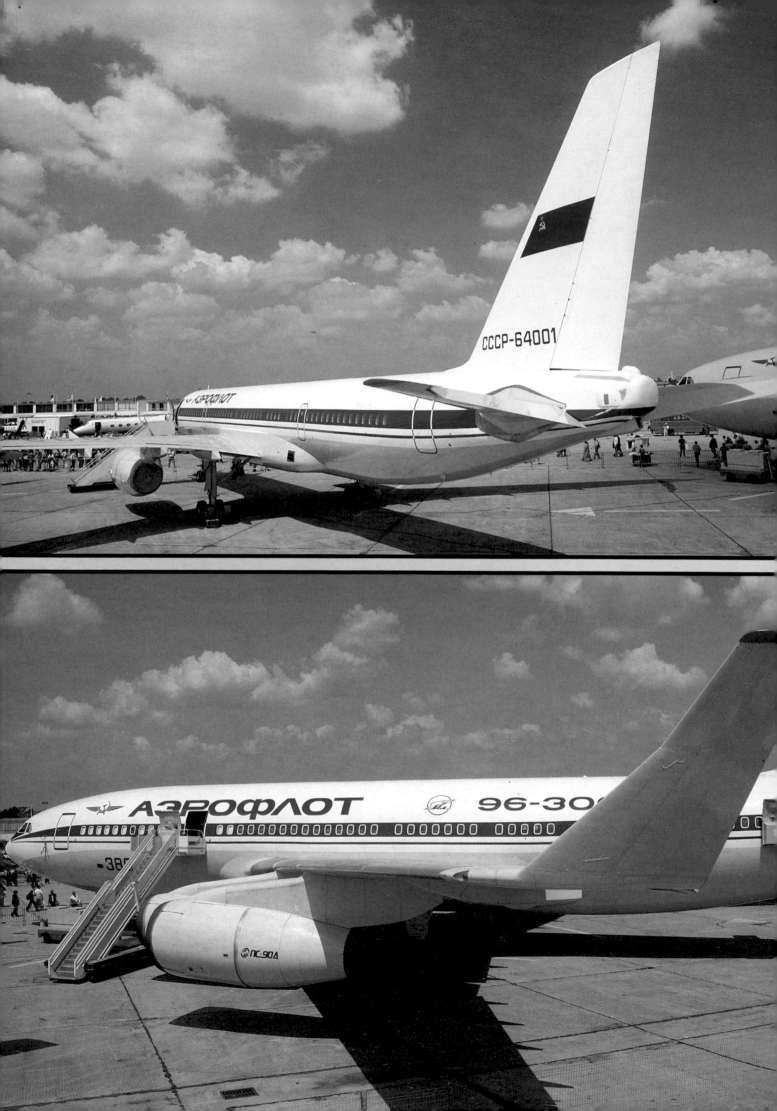

first flight on 2 January 1989 and this also represents a milestone in Soviet civil aviation – being the Soviet Union's first airliner with fly-by-wire control system, totally without mechanical connection between cockpit and control surfaces. The flightdeck features electronic flight data instrumentation displayed on six four-colour screens and pilot control inputs are via rams-horn-shaped controllers. The digital fly-by-wire system is the most advanced feature of any Soviet airliner, working on all three axes, pitch, roll and yaw, similar to that in the A320 Airbus. Although the Tu-204 is designed for a two-crew operation, provision is made for a flight engineer and it is probable that Aeroflot will elect to operate in this latter mode. Seating is for up to 214 passengers in a one-class layout nine abreast. As in many new western aircraft, flightdeck presentation is the so-called 'dark cockpit', indicating that when all systems are functioning normally, no status or warning lights are on. Initial flight tests are showing fuel flow in the cruise to be better by about 4% than the 3,270kg/hr predicted at the design state for the two Soloviev PS-90A turbofans, a new engine design offering comparable specific fuel consumption to the Rolls-Royce RB211-535. However, the possibility of fitting Rolls engines is under active consideration. The PS-90A is designed for a total life of 20,000hr with TBO of 7,500hr, the Tu-204 itself offering an airframe life of 45,000 flight hours, 20,000 flights or 20 years of use at an annual utilisation of up to 3,000hr. It will operate to ICAO Category IIIA automatic landing (200m RVR) plus automatic go-around with airspeed and vertical-hold. Provision is also made for ground-proximity warning, satellite navigation and collision avoidance. Aeroflot expects the Tu-204 to enter service by 1992 in order to replace current Tu-154 and some Tu-134, eventually receiving 500 aircraft. Longer-term prospects for the Tu-204 include development of a Soviet 'superfan' engine offering an estimated further 12% lower specific fuel consumption. The use of liquefied natural gas is also being studied as a fuel for the Tu-204. One suggestion that outbound trips to Siberia would be fuelled by kerosene and the return on liquefied gases which abound there. The latter would probably necessitate the fitting of underwing tanks for that purpose.

At first glance, the Ilyushin Il-96-300 may appear to be be nothing more than a modified Il-86, and whilst this is visually the case, it is actually considerably redesigned structurally. New engines, new wing and new systems throughout a shortened fuselage have been developed to produce an airbus able to offer Aeroflot a 7,000km range with up to 300 passengers. First flight of the Il-96-300 was made on 30 September 1988 and it is expected to enter service with Aeroflot in 1991, succeeding the Il-86 production. Once established with Aeroflot, consideration will be given to improving the range of the Il-86 by replacing the present NK-86 engines with the PS-90A used by both the Il-96 and Tu-204. Aside from giving this proposed Il-86M variant the desired range with better fuel economy, it will also streamline Aeroflot's maintenance structure. This is an important factor as Aeroflot becomes more cost conscious. The Il-96 has fly-by-wire controls but with mechanical backup. It is designed for a crew of three, with the flight engineer facing forward. For high-density routes the 300 passengers will be accommodated in two cabins with nine abreast seating. On international routes it is expected to accommodate 22 first class passengers six abreast, 40 business class eight abreast and 173 tourist class. Airframe life is designed for a 60,000hr life with 12,000 landings over 20 years. Possible long-term developments could be the Il-96-350, Il-96-400 versions offering increased passenger capacity, a twin-engined version

Above left:
The Tu-204, displayed for the first time at the 1989 Paris Show bears a remarkable resemblance to the Boeing 757. In service, the new twin-jet is expected to replace the long-serving Tu-154. *Allan Burney*

Below left:
Similar in outline to the Il-86, the new Il-96 has a significantly better performance through improved aerodynamics, a lighter structure, and more efficient engines. It can carry 300 passengers at ranges up to 4,856nm, more than double that possible with the earlier aircraft. *Allan Burney*

Below:
A three-view drawing of the projected Tupolev Tu-334 which is due to enter service in 1995.

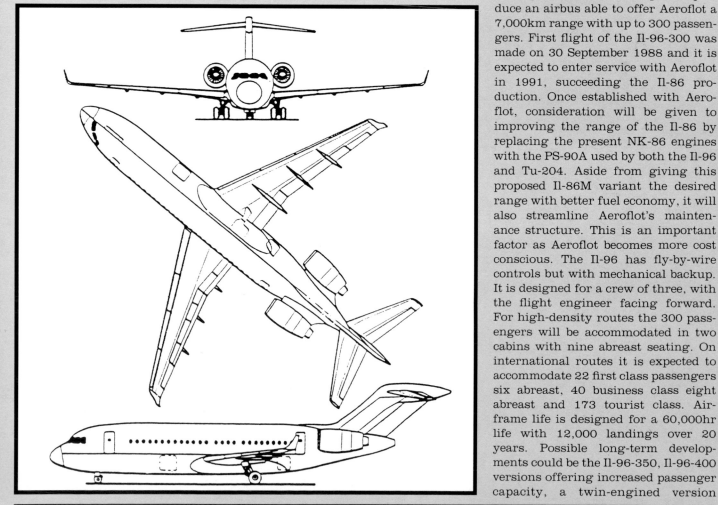

powered by a pair of Lotarev D-18 turbofans, or even the Il-96-300 with Rolls-Royce RB211s, on which there has been some discussion.

Announced in April 1989 and expected to fly in the second quarter of 1991, the Tupolev Tu-334 resembles the Fokker 100. Designed to replace the remaining Tu-134s, the Tu-334 will seat 100 passengers and will initially be built with Lotarev D-436T turbofans which are claimed to offer a 5% improvement on cruise fuel-burn of the earlier D-36 engine. This version is proposed for Aeroflot delivery in 1995. The definitive model is seen with propfan engines, giving a 50% lower fuel-burn than the turbofan model. Tupolev bureau says the Tu-334 will feature winglets, fly-by-wire systems and electronic flight instrumentation. However, by August 1989 some sources suggested the Tu-334 project would not be delivered soon enough to meet the Aeroflot domestic requirement and that the long-rumoured Yak-42M stretched (seating 156), would be reactivated.

Yakovlev Design Bureau asserts it is better suited to Aeroflot's need, will be cheaper and more reliable. The Yak-42M, if reinstated, would incorporate a host of aerodynamics and technical features not originally envisaged when it was first muted in the early 1980s.

In view of the wind of change sweeping through Aeroflot in the face of *perestroika* reforms, an outsider, but nevertheless a possibility, is the British Aerospace BAe146 powered by a pair of Lotarev turbofans. Direct purchase for hard currency would appear out of the question, but it is quite feasible given the opportunity, that the BAe146 could successfully fill a niche on Aeroflot's network. Time will tell.

Aside from passenger jets, Aeroflot operates a large fleet of several hundred Ilyushin Il-76 cargo transports on domestic and international freight services and charter flights. Il-76T, Il-76TD, Il-76M and Il-76MD variants may be encountered around the world, including the polar

regions. A large part of this fleet, in Aeroflot colours, is operated on behalf of the armed forces. In its civilian role (it joined Aeroflot in 1975), it is powered by four Soloviev D-30KP turbofans and has a range of up to 5,000km with 40 tonnes of cargo. It is very similar in configuration and size to the Lockheed C-141.

Conversion of a few early model Tu-154s to the cargo role, with Boeing 707C-style fuselage loading door, was undertaken in 1983, This conversion being designated Tu-154S.

For specialised tasks, the much smaller Antonov An-74 is employed, mostly for polar ice patrol and for some geological survey work. The type approximates to the Boeing YC-14, with two Lotarev D-36 turbofans it has good characteristics and STOL capability.

At the smallest end of the cargo fleet is the Yak-40K, which is simply the standard Yak-40 airframe with large loading door in fuselage side. It serves the more remote and mountainous areas of the Soviet Union.

At the other extreme, the Antonov An-124 Ruslan became available to Aeroflot during early 1986, with around 15 of the type on strength. Similar to the Lockheed C-5 Galaxy but slightly larger, it features the same style of upward-hinging nose section and rear loading ramp, allowing loading from both ends simultaneously. Its construction involves much advanced technology with substantial use of composites and with titanium floor, fly-by-wire controls and four Lotarev D-18T turbofans. Cargo hold capacity is 150 tonnes and the upper deck can seat 88 passengers. Flight range with a full 150 tonnes cargo load is 4,500km, but maximum flight range possible is 16,500km. Maximum take-off weight is a staggering 405 tonnes. The An-124 provides Aeroflot with unique cargo capacity for out-sized loads.

By the mid-1990s, Aeroflot will have gone a long way towards satisfying the huge domestic demand with its increased capacity types and will be operating a modern jet fleet. Many of the new aircraft will be comparable to their equivalent Western types and it will be interesting to see if the Soviet aircraft industry can make a sales breakthrough to Western airlines. In the meantime, Aeroflot has already ordered the Airbus A310 and has announced plans to set up a number of regional airlines — reversing its previous monopoly position. The face of Soviet aviation will change dramatically in the next few years!

Below:
Although basically a military freighter, the Il-76 is flown in large numbers by Aeroflot for the carriage of freight on international and domestic routes.
R. Ruffle Archives

Bottom:
The Antonov An-124 can carry a 150,000kg payload and at least 10 are believed to be in Aeroflot service. This example was photographed when visiting Heathrow in December 1988 to pick up supplies for victims of the Armenian earthquake disaster.
R. Ruffle Archives

Canadian Colours

Above:
Canada is considerably larger than the United States and, although it has a much smaller population, air transport plays a vital role in maintaining communications throughout the country. The national carrier is Air Canada, recently privatised following the sale of a government 55% shareholding, whose fleet currently includes six Boeing 747s. *Boeing*

Below:
Air Canada has a total of 21 Boeing 767-200 in service or on order, including seven extended-range versions. As part of a major re-equipment programme, the airline has also ordered 34 Airbus A320 with deliveries starting in 1990. *Boeing*

Left:
The Boeing 727 is still one of the workhorses of the Air Canada fleet with 33 in service in 1989. However, it will eventually be replaced on some routes as the new A320s enter service. *Boeing*

Below:
Canadian Airlines International, the country's second largest airline, was formed in 1987 by the merger of Canadian Pacific and Pacific Western Airlines. Its long-range fleet consists of DC-10 Srs 30 and Boeing 767 aircraft. One of the latter is shown on departure from Toronto. *R. Shaw*

Right:
Canadian Airlines Boeing 767s on the ground at Toronto's Lester B. Pearson International Airport. *R. Shaw*

Left:
The bulk of Canadian Airlines fleet is made up of the Boeing 737-200 with no less than 66 in service. They are mainly used on domestic and North American routes. *R. Shaw*

Right:
One of several airlines wearing the Canadian Airlines livery, Ontario Express is a 'Canadian Partner' and flies feeder services to Toronto from 14 points in Canada and the US. It has a fleet of eight ATR42-300 and 13 Jetstream 31 in service or on order. One of the latter is shown on approach at Toronto.

Right:
Once independent Wardair was acquired by PWA Corporation, Canadian Airline's parent company, in 1989. Since then it has abandoned most of its charter programme to UK regional airports and is concentrating on the scheduled business market using modern aircraft such as this Airbus A310-300. However, current plans call for the sale of the A310s in order to rationalise the PWA fleet. *L. Marriott*

Above:
Wardair's withdrawal from the holiday charter business provided an opening for a new carrier, Odyssey International, which was set up in 1989 to fly transatlantic charters using a fleet of three Boeing 757-200ER. Unfortunately, the airline went out of business in 1990 due to the collapse of its parent company, Soundair. *L. Marriott*

Right:
Founded in 1974, Worldways Canada is a charter airline with a fleet of four DC-8 Srs 63 and four L1011 TriStars including this example, C-GIES. *L. Marriott*

Below:
A Worldways DC-8 Srs 63, C-FCPS, taxies past two Air Ontario Dash 8s at Toronto. Despite their age, the airline's DC-8s still give good service, carrying up to 250 passengers on transatlantic charters. *R. Shaw*

Above:
Air Ontario is a major Canadian regional airline, 75% owned by Air Canada. It operates a mixed fleet which includes 25 of the Dash 8-100 shown here and has nine stretched 48-seater Dash 8-300 on order. The airline's route network forms part of the 'Air Canada Connector' system. *R. Shaw*

Left:
The turboprop-powered Convair 580 is still popular with many smaller Canadian airlines. This example, C-FARO, is one of two operated by Toronto-based Air Niagara. *R. Shaw*

Below:
Despite the influx of modern types such as the Dash 8, ATR42 and Fokker F27, the DC-3 still soldiers on. Northwest Territorial Airways is based at Yellowknife and has a fleet of five DC-3 and three L188c Electras. Propliners still rule! *R. Shaw*

EROPS - extended range operations

Leo Marriott *explores the variety of ways in which EROPS is affecting airline services*

EVER SINCE commercial air transport got into its stride after the end of World War 2, the concept of long-range over-water flights has been synonymous with large multi-engined aircraft. To a certain extent one dictated the other — long-range required a lot of fuel which in turn required a considerable amount of power to lift into the air. These requirements could only be contained in a large airframe, especially if a worthwhile payload was to be carried, and so airliners designed for transatlantic and similar routes grew inexorably in size and weight. An important factor which contributed to this escalation was the perceived safety factor in multi-engined aircraft

— four engines offered a greater reserve of power in the event of a single failure and in the days of propeller-driven aircraft this was literally a matter of life and death.

In modern times, the reliability of jet engines, particularly the big turbofans which first entered service in the early-1970s, have altered perceptions of what constitutes an acceptable risk

of engine failure. The DC-10 and Lockheed TriStar were the first modern three-engined aircraft designed for long-range intercontinental flights and they soon found a ready acceptance amongst the travelling public owing to their high standards of comfort and good safety records. With engines such as the RB211 offering in excess of 40,000lb

Below:
An Air 2000 Boeing 757 starts up for a flight to Bangor, on the United States east coast carrying a full load of British holidaymakers. *L. Marriott*

Above right:
It is not only British airlines that take advantage of the EROPS twinjets. This single Boeing 767-200ER, flown by Air Seychelles, is in regular use carrying visitors from the UK and other points to the Islands in the Indian Ocean. *Boeing*

thrust each, the consequences of a single-engine failure were minimal and the aircraft could safely fly considerable distances on the two remaining engines if required. In the event, the reliability of these big fanned engines was such that an in-flight failure was almost unheard of. Their excellent specific fuel consumption meant that the total fuel burn on a typical transatlantic flight was considerably less than would have been the case if they had been powered by four older generation engines.

The increasing power and reliability of the large turbofans led directly to a new generation of large twin-engined airliners. Surprisingly, it was the European aerospace industry which led the way with the highly successful Airbus programme and the prototype A300 first took to the air in 1972. The American industry, busy with an established line of products, was slow to respond and neither Lockheed nor McDonnell Douglas became involved in a direct conflict with the Airbus range. However, after extensive market research and much procrastination, Boeing eventually took the plunge and went ahead with two designs — the 200-seater 757 and the

290-seater wide bodied 767. First flights of these aircraft were in 1982 and 1981 respectively. By this time Airbus also had its new A310 on offer.

In the early 1980s, the airline industry was in one of its periods of recession and consequently there was cut-throat competition between Boeing and Airbus to sell its very similar aircraft. Both sets of aircraft were designed originally for European or US transcontinental routes and Airbus was also particularly successful in the southeast Asia market. However, both manufacturers could see that the market for its aircraft could be immeasurably improved if they could be used for long-distance over-water flights.

From a technical point of view, this was perfectly possible. Long-range versions of all the new twinjets were designed, taking advantage of the continuing improvement in engine performance and fuel economy offered by the three main engine manufacturers — Rolls-Royce, Pratt & Whitney and General Electric. However, it was not merely a question of building aircraft which could fly long distances with a full payload. In addition, it was necessary to convince the various national airworthiness authorities and, most importantly, the travelling public, that the operation of such aircraft could be carried out with the same standards of safety as comparable multi-engined types.

Prior to the advent of the big fanned twins, the rules governing over-water operations varied from country to country. For instance, the US FAA originally prescribed that no twin-engine aircraft (piston or jet) should be flown such that it was more than 60min flying time at single-engine speed from an airfield. This rule was originally intended to cover piston-engined aircraft and exemptions were later granted to some US twinjet operators on trans-Caribbean routes whereby the 60min stipulation was increased to 75 and then 85min.

At the same time, the International Civil Aviation Organisation (ICAO) insisted that any aircraft operating an over-water route should be able to make a suitable airport within 90min flying time after the failure of *two* engines. This rule was obviously framed for four-engined aircraft and effectively ruled out twins and trijets, although it was later modified to allow operation of the latter. Convincing the various airworthiness authorities to change these rules for the benefit of the new twinjets was a difficult but necessary exercise and involved not

Top:
Until recently long-range commercial flights have been the exclusive preserve of large multi-engined aircraft such as this Boeing 747-230B. *Lufthansa*

Above:
International Civil Aviation Organisation safety regulations for long-range over-water flights were originally drawn up to cover piston-engined aircraft and were substantially unaltered when turboprop and, eventually, jet aircraft came into service. This Britannia was required to be able to fly for 90min after 'losing' two engines. *British Airways*

Above:
The use of the wide bodied TriStar and DC-10 trijets required changes in operating regulations to permit transoceanic flights. These aircraft, together with the Boeing 747 were instrumental in proving the reliability of modern big-fanned jet engines. *TWA*

Top:
Boeing's twinjets, the 757 and 767, first flew almost 10 years after the European Airbus A300 but both manufacturers now offer extended-range versions of their aircraft.

Above:
The Boeing 767-300ER features a fourth electrical generator powered by a hydraulic motor, increased fire suppression in the cargo holds and additional equipment overheat detectors. All this is necessary to comply with FAA rules for EROPS.
Boeing

only the aircraft and engine manufacturers, but also the airlines themselves.

The prime factor was engine performance and in particular the in-flight shutdown rate demonstrated in service by each particular engine type and variant. Before any approval for EROPS could be given it was necessary for data to be available on which a decision could be based and operating criteria defined. In 1984, ICAO set up a data-gathering exercise in co-operation with airlines and manufacturers and the results of this continuing exercise have led to today's operating criteria. Basically, these are that an engine type must have demonstrated an in-service shutdown rate of less than 1 per 20,000 flights in order to be certified for a 120min dispensation. A comparable figure of less than 1 per 50,000 flights has been suggested for a 180min dispensation which is now being sought by some American airlines for trans-Pacific flights.

At present, a 90min exemption, based on the old ICAO standard, is regarded as the initial target for any airline or aircraft wishing to qualify for EROPS. However, several authorities, including the British CAA, will certify up to 120min, subject to satisfactory operating practices. In fact the UK has gone further and allows several airlines an extra 15% margin, permitting flights up to 138min flying time from a suitable airport. This was specifically done to eliminate a small triangular 'no go' area in mid-Atlantic so that the British airlines can now fly direct services from UK airports to eastern seaboard destinations in North America. It is unlikely that there will be a requirement in the foreseeable future from many British operators to go to the 180min exemptions (an option the FAA is considering for American airlines) as transatlantic and Far East routes can all be accommodated in the 138min limit.

For UK airlines, the CAA criteria for EROPS is set out in its publication CAP513 and this is concerned not only with engine performance and

reliability but covers many other factors as well. For example, tighter maintenance and inspection procedures are specified for EROPS aircraft while the list of minor equipment unserviceabilities, which would be allowable in normal operations, is considerably reduced. In the event of a single-engine failure, the remaining unit will have to run for prolonged periods at high power settings and the ability to do this must have been demonstrated during the manufacturer's test programme.

With only a single engine running, there must be sufficient electrical and hydraulic power, with redundant capacity, for normal operation. This means that an EROPS aircraft must be fitted with additional pumps, generators and auxiliary power units (APU) in order to cope with this demand. Such equipment must be capable of being started following long periods of cold soak at altitude. The rival manufacturers often adopt a different

approach to meet these specifications. For example, Boeing twins are equipped with APUs which run throughout the flight while Airbus has modified the APU and its intake to allow a cold start in flight.

Another requirement concerns the provision of better onboard fire suppression equipment. A cargo-hold fire, for instance, need only be contained for a relatively short period on a conventional flight where a landing at a diversion airfield can normally be made within 60min or less. On an EROPS flight, the fire may need to be contained for up to 3hr and consequently, the scale of onboard equip-

ment for the detection, suppression and containment of cargo hold fires, is considerably increased. Interestingly, these improvements are now being specified for multi-engined aircraft because of the inherent increase in safety in such measures.

By the late-1980s, the manufacturers and airlines had satisfied the various certifying authorities and the first commercial EROPS flights were started. In the UK, the emphasis until recently has been on transatlantic charter flights and, in 1989, there were four operators on these routes — Britannia Airways, Monarch, Air 2000 and Air Europe. Except for

Britannia, which flies Boeing 767s, all these airlines use modern Boeing 757s fitted with Rolls-Royce engines. These flights have transformed the UK holiday market and exotic destinations such as Florida, Santa Domingo, Montego Bay and Barbados are now a viable alternative to the crowded Mediterranean resorts. In addition, flights across the Atlantic are rarely subject to the long delays which have become the norm in Europe.

A typical operator is Air 2000 which flies from Gatwick, Manchester and Glasgow with its 757s. Although serving a variety of destinations including Orlando and the Caribbean islands, most of its flights are routed via Bangor in the US State of Maine, on the northeastern American seaboard. A typical flight time from the UK to Bangor is 6hr 50min and a short technical stop is made here before flying on to the final destination. While the aircraft is being turned round, the passengers are disembarked and are able to go through US customs formalities — quickly done at this relatively quiet airport and avoiding the notorious problems at crowded gateways such as Orlando and Miami. It is interesting to note the great circle distances involved in these Air 2000 flights which are routinely flown without incident.

Manchester to Bangor, Me	2,581nm
Glasgow to Bangor, Me	2,469nm
Gatwick to Bangor, Me	2,695nm
Orlando to Manchester	3,687nm

Owing to the favourable wind patterns, return flights to the UK are often made directly from Orlando. For the airline's crews to be permitted to fly these routes, they must undergo additional training on a three-day ground course covering weather planning minima, technical features of the EROPS aircraft and use of additional safety equipment. Within 90 days of this course and written examination, they must make their first EROPS flight and subsequently fly two Atlantic and two North American sectors under the supervision of a Training Captain before being qualified. Additional engineering and maintenance facilities have been set up at Bangor in order to cope with the requirements of EROPS flights. These are shared with Air Europe which also operates similar flights using Bangor. The mass arrival of British holidaymakers passing through Bangor must have provided a welcome source

Above:
Austrian Airlines has two Airbus A310-300 with a third on order for delivery in 1991. These are currently used for direct flights from Vienna to New York.
Austrian Airlines

of revenue to an airport which otherwise was 'off the beaten track' as far as transatlantic flights were concerned.

Air 2000 already has approval for EROPS within 138min of a suitable airfield but is currently awaiting CAA approval for operations up to 180min — the RB211-535-E4 engine fitted to its aircraft is already cleared to this limit.

Flying the larger Boeing 767, Britannia Airways launched its inaugural EROPS flights in November 1988 — in the other direction. Heading east and south, the airline pioneered a programme of charter flights to Australia. Despite some doubts in the travel industry, these flights have been very successful and, in 1989, Britannia announced an increased programme which also added New Zealand to the list of antipodean destinations. In April 1989, the airline also joined the rush to the North Atlantic with flights from Gatwick, Luton and Manchester to Orlando, Montego Bay, Barbados and Acapulco.

Although the UK emphasis has, so far, been on EROPS flights by charter operators, the Atlantic routes are also served by an increasing number of scheduled airlines using twinjets. Typical of these is Wardair with Airbus A310s and TWA, American Airlines and Delta with Boeing 767s. British Airways will soon join the fray as its new 767s are delivered. The use of economic twinjets on the North Atlantic routes has a number of spin-offs which all act in favour of the customer. For a start fare levels can be kept reasonably low while still providing adequate operating revenue for the airline. The use of smaller aircraft means that frequencies can be increased, improving the viability of long-range scheduled services from regional airports rather than congested major hubs such as Heathrow. In particular Manchester has benefitted from the introduction of the transatlantic services using EROPS twins, and Glasgow looks set to follow now that Government policy allows scheduled transatlantic flights to use the airport instead of Prestwick.

Nor is this trend confined to the UK. Many European airlines are adding twinjets to the fleet to take advantage of their flexibility and operating economics. SAS for instance has 13 Extended Range 767s on order and will use these for flights as far afield as Rio de Janeiro (already served from the UK by Monarch Airlines' Boeing 757s). Even small airlines are able to consider long range routes. A good example is Austrian Airlines which commenced direct flights from Vienna to New York in March 1989 using an Airbus A310 configured to seat 172 passengers. Even more exotically it flies to Tokyo via Moscow, the crew being supplemented by a Soviet navigator for the Moscow-Tokyo leg (strictly speaking this is not an EROPS route as most of the flight is overland, but it illustrates the tremendous flexibility offered by these aircraft).

The full effect of EROPS on the world airline scene has yet to be appreciated but already some fundamental changes in the structure and pricing of services can be seen. In the 1990s, EROPS twinjets will bring intercontinental travel to an infinitely greater number of people than has ever been the case in the past. The world will undoubtedly seem an even smaller place in years to come.

757 DELIVERY

Many readers will be familiar with the pleasant sensation of being handed the keys of a new car and driving away in it — but what is it like to be given the keys of a brand new airliner straight off the production line? **Philip Domogala** *had just such an experience when he was invited to take delivery of a Boeing 757-200 at Seattle for the German charter airline LTU Sud*

Above:
LTU Sud, founded in 1983, is a sister company to LTU (*Lufttransport Unternehmen KG***) and operates a fleet of seven Boeing 757-200s from southern Germany. Originally known as LTS, the new style title and a revised livery were adopted in 1988. This is one of the airline's 757s in the original blue and white colour scheme.**
Boeing

RECEIVING THE 'KEYS' of a new aeroplane at Boeing used to be a big ceremony. However, with the boom in the aviation industry and the increased production rate which has resulted, Boeing sometimes hands over up to five aircraft in one day. The event is still an emotional moment, especially for the receiving airline, and Boeing tries to keep it that way. Nevertheless, one can still feel the pressure of the next customer waiting in line behind you!

We arrived at Seattle on 1 May 1989 to hear that the LTU aircraft would be delayed for about two days owing to 'unforeseen circumstances'. These circumstances were that the receiving airline pilots, our LTU friends, had found a list of 'little things' that needed to be fixed before the aircraft could be accepted. This rectification programme had overrun but at least it gave us ample time to visit Seattle and its surroundings, as well as the massive Boeing factories scattered around the city.

Boeing's current production concentrates on the models 737, 747, 757 and 767 and this is split between Renton, where the narrow-bodied 737 and 757 are produced, and Everett, some 30 miles north of Seattle which is home to the production of the wide-bodied 747 and 767. The factory at Everett is famed as the largest enclosed structure in the world and was specially built as part of the 747 programme in the late-1960s.

The narrow-body plant at Renton is 10 miles south of Seattle and is the site of much of Boeing's early history. The pioneering 707 was built here, followed by the highly successful three-engined 727 and currently the various versions of the 737 and the 757. Although production of the 727 has now ceased, the 707 line is still open for special orders for aircraft such as the AWACS, the E-3 and KC-135 tankers — all of which are based on the tried and tested 707 airframe. However, most of the production work now concentrates on the current 737 and 757 and this is where 'our' 757 was born.

A look around the production line quickly reveals that the 757 is not actually manufactured at Renton — it is just assembled there. The four million or so components are manu-factured around the world by companies in Japan and Europe, as well as the US, although Boeing does manufacture some electrical equipment and interior cabin panels in Seattle.

The parts, components and completed structures come by various forms of transportation including sea containers, railway, air cargo and road trucks, and are then checked thoroughly for quality by Boeing inspectors. Once accepted, the parts are numbered for future reference and distributed to the production line where 'new' aircraft are assembled.

It takes about four weeks for the aircraft to be assembled in the hangar up to the point where it can roll on its own wheels. It is then waterproofed and moved outside where another four or five weeks elapse while the airframe is fitted out and the engines mounted — in our case, Rolls-Royce RB211-E4 from Great Britain.

Once completed, a Boeing pilot and engineer will carry out preliminary tests and ground runs before making

the maiden flight. Normally, a total of four or five flights will be necessary in order to clear the aircraft for delivery. The first flight is designated B1, Boeing's first flight, and this is followed by B2 to check that any problems thrown up on the initial sortie have been corrected. B3 is generally a flight conducted by an FAA check pilot in order to clear the aircraft for a Certificate of Airworthiness to cover the delivery flight. If all has gone well up to this stage, the aircraft is handed over to the customer's pilots or representative for a short series of flights commencing with C1. If any problems are highlighted, these will be rectified and checked in a subsequent flight — this process being repeated until the customer is happy and is willing to accept the aircraft.

In our case, this process had taken a little longer than anticipated and hence the two-day delay. Finally, on 5 May 1989, the LTU aircraft was on the tarmac in front of the Boeing Flight Centre at Seattle's Boeing Field and ready for its delivery flight to Munich. It already proudly bore its new German registration, D-AMUM, and our departure was planned for the early afternoon.

With the help of a couple of Boeing engineers, we opened the underside cargo doors and loaded our few bags into the brand new and unmarked compartment. On the flightdeck, our American captain (an ex-Boeing test pilot) was already busy running through the pre-flight checks and signing the final paperwork. However, before starting up he carried out a very thorough and lengthy external and internal inspection of the aircraft before giving a final 'OK' to the relieved Boeing engineers.

Our aircraft was one of three being delivered to customers that day, the other two being a 737-400 for Icelandair and a 757-200 for an 'unspecified' customer. We were second in line at the official handover ceremony and were intrigued to see that the secret customer was in fact Air 3000, a brand new airline. Each handover ceremony lasted about 20min and after the usual photo session, we were free to leave.

We boarded the aircraft which was fitted with only a few Boeing-supplied seats in the main cabin — just enough for the members of the delivery party. The final fitting out of the interior

would be carried out at LTU Sud's home base. The planned flight time from Seattle to Munich is an amazing 9hr 45min. It is easy to forget that Seattle is a long way north and consequently the great circle route over the Arctic is not as long as might be thought. There is also a friendly 100kt tailwind for much of the flight.

The inside of the aircraft smells of new plastic, just like a new car, and also of oil and grease from several points in the unfitted interior. However this soon wears off and after a couple of hours and a few cigarettes it smells like any other aircraft. After finally closing the doors the engines are started although our conscientious captain has more power checks to complete before being satisfied that we are ready to go.

Eventually we take off and climb steeply to our cruising level, 37,000ft. Our route takes us northeast from Seattle, and Vancouver is just visible in the distance off to port as we climb over Canada and then head out over Edmonton to the 'white desert' of the Canadian Northern Territories. From above, on a sunny afternoon, it looks

like the end of the world — hundreds of miles of frozen land and lakes, all snow covered. There is no sign of trees or human habitation as we cross Hudson Bay and Baffin Island before crossing a short stretch of sea en route to Greenland. On the flightdeck the compass shows that we are now heading southeast, although we have hardly altered course since leaving Seattle. Navigation in this part of the world is a revelation to those of us used to looking at flat maps with north at the top.

Having burnt off a fair amount of fuel, the aircraft is considerably lighter and we climb to 41,000ft. Shortly afterwards we pass over Rekyavik in Iceland, then the Shetland Islands and Scotland. By the time we cross over Amsterdam we have climbed still further, to 43,000ft, but then it is time to commence the long descent into Munich where we land at 10.00hr in the morning (local time). Amazingly, we realise that the whole flight has been conducted in daylight, having travelled so far north that at this time of the year the sun never dipped below the horizon.

After our arrival it is business as usual. By now the aircraft has amassed some 15hr flying time since new and the LTU hangar staff surround the aircraft as they begin to prepare to transform it into a normal airliner. Within 48hr, it will be fully fitted out and ready to fly its first revenue earning flight — a charter to Las Palmas. We all left the aircraft thinking that it was a unique example, but very soon it will be just another 757 amongst the crowded skies and airports of Europe.

Heathrow - world cargocentre

Philip Birtles *looks at the increasing importance of Heathrow as a world cargocentre*

LONDON HEATHROW is well known as Britain's premier gateway for airline passengers, but what is less obvious is the importance of its air cargo operations. In a vast cargo area on the southwest corner of Heathrow is BAA Air Cargo, which receives some 20 regular cargo scheduled carriers, and up to 40 non-scheduled operators. Among the regular operators are Lufthansa, Finnair and Air France, with Cathay Pacific operating cargo flights only into Heathrow (its passenger operations being from Gatwick and Manchester). The one dedicated scheduled cargo airline operating into Heathrow is Federal Express, which took over the Flying Tiger operations.

The cargo area is laid out with three parallel lines of freight sheds, two lines facing each other across the airside apron and the third separated from the middle one by the landside loading bays and a car park. A further line of cargo sheds is used exclusively by British Airways, but does not have airside parking for aircraft, as the buildings are used for build-up and breakdown of cargo pallets for the underfloor holds of the BA scheduled

services from the normal passenger terminals. A wide-bodied airliner's economics are greatly improved by filling the hold with air cargo in addition to the passenger baggage.

Air cargo began at Heathrow as the embryo airport was finding its feet after World War 2. Capt Don Bennett, of RAF Bomber Command Pathfinder fame, captained a British South American Airways Avro Lancastrian, on an initial proving flight, leaving

Below:
Singapore Airlines Boeing 747-212F, 9V-SKQ, is a regular visitor to the Heathrow World cargocentre. *Boeing*

Top:
The great majority of air cargo travels in and out of Heathrow in the underfloor cargo holds of the regular passenger schedules.

Above:
Flying Tiger also operated a number of converted passenger aircraft.

Heathrow on 1 January 1946 bound for Buenos Aires. Cargo operations grew slowly using a variety of sheds and facilities around the airport until, in 1969, the dedicated Heathrow World Cargocentre was opened. As the capacity increased, companies began moving into this cargo facility, not only to handle the dedicated airfreight aircraft, but also the underfloor cargo on the passenger aircraft. This was made a great deal easier by the construction of a tunnel from the southside cargo centre to the central area. This reduced journey times from the cargo shed to the aircraft on stand to an average of 10min.

London Airport and its cargo operations play a vital part in the overall British economy. Goods need to be moved quickly and efficiently, especially if they are perishable or of high value. It is of little use transporting products by air for greater speed if the port of arrival or depar-

ture cannot handle the cargo efficiently. Britain's economy is dependent upon its export trade, and in a highly competitive world market, there is a vital need for an effective distribution network. BAA Air Cargo is a principle gateway to the world through its major cargo centres at Heathrow, Gatwick and Stansted. Between the three airports, they handle more than 15% of the total value of Britain's visible trade, worth more than £24 million per year.

The efficient distribution of cargo is made a great deal easier owing to London's airports offering more flights to more destinations than any other city in the world. London also offers a greater choice of carriers and agents, the majority of which are linked into the highly sophisticated ACP90 computerised cargo system.

Air cargo has often been regarded as the 'poor relation' of the air transport industry, but without it many passen-

ger services would not be viable. Although air cargo may account for only about 1% of worldwide cargo movements by volume, it gains on the overall high value of the goods. Air cargo can provide between 15 and 25% of the airline revenue, and often a higher proportion of its profit, probably making the vital difference between success and failure. Passenger and cargo activities are totally complimentary with around 85% of all Heathrow's cargo movements going in the hold of passenger aircraft.

The largest single air cargo operator at Heathrow is British Airways, with its own 33-acre site optimised for handling freight for the hold of passenger aircraft, since the airline withdrew from pure cargo operations some years ago. Since 1983, BA has been gearing up its cargo centre to handle more freight, more efficiently, and the merger with British Caledonian Airways came at a time when the multi-million pound development programme was nearly complete. This allowed a rapid merger of the cargo business and provided BA with the facilities of the ex-British Caledonian 54,000sq ft Heathrow transit shed close by to the BA cargo centre. This is run as a self-contained business to handle the third party contract work. Until the merger, BA had handled about a dozen foreign airlines at its cargo centre, but from mid-1988 this was merged with the half-dozen or so ex-BCal customers to form a dedicated business. This gave a clearer focus on the market place without split loyalties with BA's own cargo business. The management of the third party unit have the authority to make their own business judgements and seek out new opportunities. This gives BA Cargo the chance to concentrate exclusively on its own product lines.

Over a two-year period, BA has invested over £10 million in the Cargocentre, including: doubling the size of the elevating transfer vehicle (ETV) to handle a potential throughput of 7,500 tonnes a week; computerising and increasing the volume of the loose cargo storage area to 6,000 cells; and an improved truck handling system. The acquisition of BCal by British Airways boosted BA Cargo business by £100 million, to a £400 million per year turnover. Tonnage throughput at the BA Cargo Centre is in excess of 270,000 tonnes per year, with traffic increasing significantly.

In addition to the major investment in new equipment to improve reliability, a significant investment is made in the work force where the wage bill is in excess of £15 million per year. It is considered vital that the work force is highly motivated and their flexibility is tuned to the customers' needs.

The world's largest all-cargo carrier, Flying Tiger lost its well established identity in August 1989, when it was absorbed by Federal Express. After some 43 years of operation, Flying Tigers had had varied fortunes, 1986 being almost the end of the airline owing to mounting losses and a drop in market share. However, the company bounced back with record profits the following year, becoming a lean and hungry carrier. In 1988, the airline was presented with the airport's first 'Airline of the Year' award in recognition of its outstanding cargo operations.

Flying Tiger was the only all-cargo scheduled operator into Heathrow, flying regular daily routes from New York to Heathrow and Frankfurt using Boeing 747s, some converted from passenger aircraft and other dedicated nose-loaders for bulky freight. The average load of a converted 747-100 is around 100 tonnes

Top:
The inside of the 747 freighter lacks the normal passenger facilities with sidewall protection against damage by the cargo loads. The floor is covered with the cargo handling system for either pallet loads or containers in two lines.

Below:
Japan Airlines operates nose-loading Boeing 747 freighters in a basic livery without company titles.

Above:
Cargo Airlines of Israel is the El Al air cargo operator, devoid of company titles, although the basic livery is easily recognisable.

Top:
Air Canada Cargo Express operates DC-8 Srs 73AF C-FTIS powered by the quieter, more economical CFM56 engines.

Above:
TMA of the Lebanon operates the all-cargo Boeing 707s converted from passenger service, in the case of OD-AGS being ex-TWA.

and the -200, 120 tonnes. The ex-passenger aircraft has a rear upward opening cargo door on the port side behind the wing trailing edge and the whole aircraft floor is roller-matted for each cargo movement with minimum effort.

Loads can either be in standard igloo containers or pallets lashed down and polythene sheeted. All pallet building is handled by what is now Federal Express to ensure that the cargo load is safe, and also not of a hazardous nature, unless proper precautions are taken. The minimum headroom is dictated not only by the cargo door, but the clearance under the forward upper deck.

Although a freight 747 looks fairly conventional from the outside, it is hardly what a passenger would expect inside. The majority of the windows are blanked over inside and all the trim is removed, giving an idea of the overall volume inside the fuselage without the usual cabin roof and overhead bins. The insulation is still present since air-conditioning and pressurisation are required for cargos of livestock, as well as crew comfort. The crew compartment on the top deck is somewhat spartan, with a few seats for any attendants for live cargo. Passengers are not carried at all. Although lower deck cargo space is

available, the major part of the load is on the upper deck where the handling systems make it easier to deal with, specifically to speed the turnround.

The Federal Express facility at Heathrow covers around 40,000sq ft and employs over 100 people. When not dealing with its own cargo fleet, it handles the cargo services of other major international airlines, including TAP Air Portugal and THY Turkish Airlines, as well as a number of *ad hoc* assignments.

An example of a regular international airline actively selling its cargo space is Air-India, creating a growing demand for air cargo operations from Britain. The Indian government's policy of easing the trade barriers to allow import of the high tech equipment so vital to the efficient operation of its industry, has brought an increased demand for air cargo services. The airline has introduced a pair of Boeing 747-300 Combis to increase capacity to 271 passengers and seven cargo pallets on

the main deck. However, following the loss of the South African Airways 747 Combi off Mauritius with a fire in a suspect cargo, the use of combined main deck cargo and passenger carrying has been restricted pending tougher regulations. The underfloor cargo capacity is normally four pallets and 18 containers. As well as flying from Europe to India, the cargo services have also been extended to Japan, and the airline normally operates at least one cargo flight out of London every week.

KLM Royal Dutch Airlines has recently doubled the cargo capacity of its warehouse at Heathrow by an investment of £5 million to cope with the increased business demand.

Aer Lingus has based cargo operations at Heathrow for over 25 years and its throughput has risen within a year by some 25% to over 26,500 tonnes. The airline also handles the cargo requirements for a number of other airlines, both domestic and overseas.

El Al operates all cargo 747-100s under the name Cargo Airlines of Israel, but its livery is undoubtedly El Al in its basic concept, with the title of 'cargo' in place of the usual El Al markings. The airline specialises in the carriage of perishables, but it also holds the record for the largest single piece of cargo carried from Heathrow — a 51-tonne generator. A total of some 40 staff provide a round-the-clock cargo service, despite the non-operation of the airline on the Jewish Sabbath, Saturday. However, only the aircraft operations ceases for one day, while the operations continue at Heathrow with a throughput of over 25,000 tonnes per year of air cargo. Two cargo flights pass through Heathrow on each operating day from Tel Aviv, the fleet being standardised on the Boeing products, consisting of two 747 freighters, a pair of nose-loading combis, a hush-kitted 707, four 767s and two 757s.

However, London Air Cargo is not just the big operators. Air Canada Cargo Express operate its CFM56-powered stretched DC-8s, TMA of the Lebanon use venerable 707s and Air Bridge fly the prop-jet Lockheed Electra in a cargo configuration. Varig Cargo has used its DC-10 Srs 30 Freighter to carry the participating cars in the Brazilian Grand Prix, the overall variety of cargo loads demonstrating that there is not a great deal, apart from really bulky or low value cargoes which cannot take advantage of next-day delivery by air to most parts of the world.

The growth of the London airports may be visually most apparent with passengers, but air cargo is the quiet revolution with a high current growth, and further massive growth potential. Also air cargo, once loaded, tends to be much less trouble. It doesn't need a 'gang' of cabin attendants to keep it fed and 'watered', it doesn't need entertaining with movies, and it doesn't complain — other than an odd Neigh or Baa!

Above:
Air Bridge keeps the Lockheed Electra flying on commercial cargo operations on the US register, N356Q being an example.

Below:
Varig Cargo DC-10 Srs 30F has been used to transport cars to the Brazilian Grand Prix.

Rolls-Royce's big fan

Jim Cowney *visits Rolls-Royce to look a the continuing success of the RB211 engine*

SUCCESSFUL AIRCRAFT and engine programmes are now spanning much longer periods of time than in the past. An example is the Boeing 747, which entered service in 1970, but in developed form will continue to fly passengers over the world's air routes far into the next century.

The key to this longevity is the continuing improvement of a good basic design — and in the powerplant field the Rolls-Royce RB211 engine is an excellent example. Project work leading to the RB211 began early in the 1960s, the first orders for the engine were placed in 1968 and developed versions continue in production today. Orders have now been received for a version which will eventually be nearly twice as powerful as the first RB211 and it is clear that the complete life cycle of the RB211 engine family will span 60 years or

more before the last derivative RB211 is retired — far into the next century.

Today the three major versions of the RB211 in service have accumulated over 34 million hours of operating experience. Orders have been placed for more than 3,000 RB211s ranging from the 42,000lb thrust RB211-22B to the new Trent, previously known as the RB211-524L. It will provide thrusts of 67,500 to 75,000lb with eventual growth to over 80,000lb.

The RB211 has been a major success in export markets. It was designed from the start for aircraft produced outside the UK and had never been installed in a British-made aircraft,

although extensively used by British airline operators. The whole programme had provided Britain with a great deal of export business — a single RB211 for a Boeing 747-400 earns well over £4 million.

Fierce competition has come from the large turbofans produced by Pratt & Whitney and General Electric so that continued development to extend the RB211's performance has been driven by market forces. This has led to more power, better fuel consumption, reliability improvements and lower overall cost of ownership. Rolls-Royce has had to fight continually to assure the engine's commercial success and to increase its share of the

Below:
Powered by 58,000lb thrust RB211-534G engines, a Qantas Boeing 747-400 recently set a world record distance flight for an unmodified commercial aircraft by flying over 11,000 miles direct from London to Sydney.

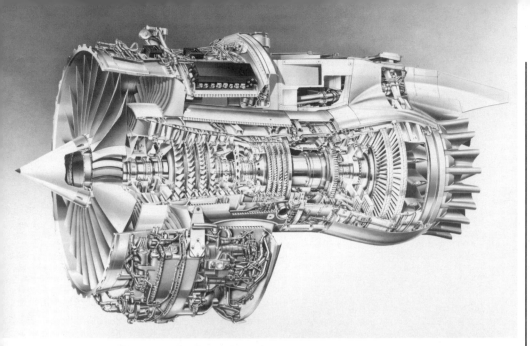

Top:
Cutaway view of the RB211-524G/H engine which powers the long-range Boeing 747-400. *All photos courtesy Rolls-Royce unless otherwise credited*

Above:
An early development RB211-06 with Hyfil carbon-fibre blades.

market for large turbofans. These efforts have been crowned with success in recent years.

The engine was launched to power the Lockheed L-1011 TriStar and Rolls-Royce succeeded in fighting off attempts by other suppliers to sell their engines for installation on the aircraft. Uniquely the TriStar is the only wide-bodied airliner to have been powered by a single type of engine — but unfortunately for Rolls-Royce it was also the first to go out of production!

Efforts to widen the market for the engine led in 1975 to the first order for RB211-powered Boeing 747s, placed by British Airways. This followed the launch of the 48,000lb-thrust RB211-524 in 1974 to power extended-range L-1011-200 TriStars ordered by Saudia.

Since 1975, the Boeing 747 has been a key application for successive versions of the engine. The latest Boeing 747, the long-range -400 variant, has been ordered by a number of operators with 58,000lb thrust RB211-524G/H engines.

In 1978 Rolls-Royce launched the lower-thrust RB211-535 to power the Boeing 757, the airliner intended to succeed the 727 which was, at that time, the best selling jet airliner ever produced. The derivative RB211-535C, providing 37,400lb take-off thrust, was ordered by Eastern Airlines and British Airways, the launch customers for the 757. Based on the engine core of the RB211-22B, but driving a lower-diameter fan, it was the first Rolls-Royce engine to be chosen as the initial powerplant for a new Boeing airliner. General Electric withdrew from the competition to power Boeing 757s, but Rolls-Royce did not remain the sole engine supplier for long. Pratt & Whitney offered a new engine, the PW2037, and it was ordered by Delta Airlines. Rolls-Royce in turn responded with a more powerful and fuel-efficient RB211-535 — the 40,100lb-thrust 535E4.

Much advanced technology was built into the RB211-535E4 and its rapid development was a major success of the RB211 programme. With excellent performance and outstanding reliability, the 535E4 has proved a worthy competitor to the PW2037 which suffered in its early years of service from the lower reliability inevitable when introducing a wholly new engine.

Well over half the engines sold for Boeing 757s have been 535E4s; in 1988 the Rolls-Royce engine accounted for 72% of powerplant sales for the aircraft. Demand for the 757 has increased in recent years and by October 1989 orders had been placed for 315 of these airliners with Rolls-Royce engines.

Growing family

By 1987 there were three main variants of the RB211 — the 42,000lb thrust RB211-22B for medium-range TriStars; the RB211-524 family for longer-range TriStars, Boeing 747s and, more recently, Boeing 767s, with thrusts from 48,000 to 60,600lb; and the RB211-535 family for Boeing 757s, providing up to 40,100lb take-off thrust.

Above:
A converted VC-10 was used as a flying testbed for the RB211 where it displaced two of the four Rolls-Royce Conway engines which normally powered this aircraft.

Technical advancement had achieved steady improvements in take-off thrusts and specific fuel consumption without the need to increase the fan diameter of RB211-524 engines. This had been possible because Rolls-Royce introduced a wide-chord fan, initially on the 535E4 and later on the most powerful -524 engines. But a larger engine was needed to provide thrusts from 65,000lb to 80,000lb and above for new wide-bodied aircraft entering service early in the 1990s — the McDonnell Douglas MD-11 and Airbus A330, as well as further developments of the Boeing 767 and Boeing 747.

To meet this need, Rolls-Royce is developing a new larger-diameter engine, the Trent (formerly known as the RB211-524L), based on experience with earlier RB211s. It incorporates the same high-pressure core as the RB211-524G/H. The launch order for 524L engines to power MD-11 airliners was announced by Air Europe early in 1989 and soon afterwards Cathay Pacific Airways announced the first order for Airbus A330s with Trent engines, followed by a similar purchase from Trans-World Airlines. By October 1989, orders and options had been placed for 174 Trent engines for 18 MD-11s and 60 A330s.

Below:
The RB211 was launched to power the Lockheed L-1011 TriStar. The prototype, powered by three RB211-22F engines, is shown taking-off for its maiden flight on 16 November 1970.

Rolls-Royce is now manufacturing or developing versions of the RB211 for five types of large commercial aircraft — the Boeing 747, 757 and 767; the MD11 and the A330.

History

American engine companies began the development of large turbofans before Rolls-Royce. In the early-1960s, Pratt & Whitney and General Electric received US government funding to design and build demonstrator versions of large high-bypass engines while Boeing and Lockheed were given contracts to evolve large airframes. These contracts were intended to demonstrate the technology needed for the C-5A military transport.

In 1965 the airframe order for the C-5A was awarded to Lockheed and the aircraft's TF39 turbofans were ordered from General Electric. Boeing and Pratt & Whitney were the losers in the C-5A competition, but worked together to apply their new technology in the civil field. This led to the launch of the Boeing 747 with its large JT9D turbofans; the first order was placed by Pan American in 1966.

Meanwhile Rolls-Royce had been studying the best type of engine to succeed its Conway turbofan, which was rated at up to 21,800lb take-off thrust. Proposals were made for the 25,000lb thrust RB178 — a two-shaft engine for long-range subsonic airliners — and in April 1965 the company's board was asked to authorise manufacture of an RB178 demonstrator rated at 28,500lb thrust.

By late-1965, Rolls-Royce market studies showed that there would be sufficient demand in the next decade to support one large engine, or possibly two. As the company studied its revolutionary three-shaft concept it became convinced that it could offer an engine with much greater thrust than the RB178 demonstrator. This first ran in July 1966, but test running was limited because costs were above budget. Thus while US companies were gaining experience with large high-bypass engines, Rolls-Royce obtained only limited test information from its lower bypass RB178. The company believed that large-diameter high-bypass engines would be too heavy and have too high an installed drag.

Rolls-Royce considered that these effects would counteract the benefits of the low testbed specific fuel consumption provided by using high-bypass ratios. (Higher propulsive efficiency is achieved with high-bypass ratios because each pound of

RB211 engines in production at Derby in 1971. At this stage the major modules have been brought together for final assembly.

thrust comes from accelerating a larger mass of air to a lower exhaust speed.) Rolls-Royce changed its views when its engine proposals were discussed with Boeing, which was confident that it could instal high-bypass turbofans in a manner which would minimise their drag. Rolls-Royce bypass ratios would have to go up to around 5:1 if its engines were to be competitive for the 747.

Rolls-Royce then submitted an engine proposal for the Boeing 747, but the Pratt & Whitney JT9D was selected. After it failed to sell the RB211 for the initial Boeing 747, the Company became progressively more keen to win a major order for the engine as it was becoming clear that large engines would account for the lion's share of the future orders for commercial engines — as they do today. Rolls-Royce proposed the development of two large new engines, both of three-shaft design — the RB207 and the RB211. The RB207 was the larger and was eventually offered at thrusts well over 50,000lb before it was abandoned. It was specified for the European Airbus in the late-1960s and proposed for the projected BAC 2-11 and twin-engined US airbuses. But by May 1967, US studies suggested that an engine of 33,000lb thrust would be needed if a three-engined US airliner was launched instead of the twin-engined types initially studied. In June, American Airlines decided in favour of a trijet rather than the big twin-engined design.

Lockheed was a potential supplier of such aircraft and in response to the request for a proposal, Rolls-Royce offered the RB211-06 engine in June 1967. Douglas was also considering a three-engined aircraft which became

the DC-10. Rated at 33,260lb thrust, the RB211-06 was an ambitious design offering high thrust, a reduction of 25% in specified fuel consumption over earlier engines and very low noise levels. It incorporated many technical advances — including a three-shaft design, use of new materials such as the Hyfil carbon-fibre composite specified for its fan blades, and an annular combustion system.

The launch order for the RB211-22 version of the engine was announced on 29 March 1968. Lockheed ordered 450 of the powerplants and at the same time Trans-World and Eastern Airlines announced orders for a total of 94 TriStars, while Air Holdings ordered 50 aircraft. By that time the take-off thrust needed had risen to 40,600lb from the 33,260 of the RB211-06. It was later raised to 42,000lb. The task of developing the RB211-22 within the required time scale was formidable. Testing of the RB211-06 began in August 1968 but costs rose rapidly. The first flight of the TriStar was preceded by engine testing in a VC10 with two of its four Conways removed and replaced by a single RB211.

The TriStar first flew on 16 November 1970 with RB211-22 engines giving 33,500lb take-off thrust. Intensive efforts continued to meet the engine's specified performance and a production programme which would allow the Tristar to enter service in December 1971 as planned. Conventional solid fan blades were installed because of problems experienced with the Hyfil blades. As the result of financial problems caused by the RB211 programme, Rolls-Royce went into receivership on 4 February 1971. Its gas turbine activities were subsequently taken over by the state-owned company Rolls-Royce (1971) Limited, but it has since returned to the private sector as Rolls-Royce plc. By coincidence, RB211 test results sent to London on 4 February 1971 showed that engine modifications were proving effective and that its thrust was approaching the required level. After a period of uncertainty, the RB211 contract was renegotiated and the TriStar entered service in April 1972, six months later than first planned.

Although the Boeing 747 first flew in 1969, it was not until 1975 that the first Rolls-Royce-powered version was ordered by British Airways. This view shows the first flight of this version in September 1976.

Although Rolls-Royce had spent more than intended, it was a major achievement to get the engine into service in early 1972 because of the difficult targets to be met. The report on events culminating in the receivership says: 'The performance of the company on the project was remarkable. The extent to which countless individuals contributed exceptional personal efforts to the task should not go unrecorded.' That dedication has continued throughout the years of the RB211 programme.

As with the other large turbofans, the RB211 took some time to achieve the levels of reliability targetted for it. Any completely new engine requires a period of years before it becomes mature and its operating costs and in-flight shutdown and unscheduled removal rates are brought down to the outstanding levels now achieved. As normally happens, the later derivative RB211s have proved much more reliable when first introduced. These benefit from all the operating experience with earlier versions and incorporate later improvements in technology. For example, the RB211-535E4 engine for the Boeing 757 established record levels of reliability and low ownership costs as soon as it entered service.

Technology advances
Considerable advances have been made in engine technology in the two decades since the early days of the RB211. These have given later versions higher performance, better fuel consumption and improved reliability. The widespread introduction of cheaper and more effective computing power has revolutionised many aspects of the business.

Above:
The RB211 has found a ready market in the Boeing 757. This example flown by America West Airlines is powered by the RB211-535E4 offering a thrust of 40,100lb and unprecedented reliability.

Below:
The Boeing 767s recently ordered by British Airways will be powered by RB211-524H engines — the first application of Rolls-Royce engines on this aircraft.

Engine components are now designed using computerised 3D gas-flow techniques, leading to new component shapes ' with better performance. Computerised design and manufacturing systems have greatly increased the efficiency of production; automated factories now manufacture engine parts. The computer has had a great impact on every aspect of the business.

RB211 improvements have been introduced after advanced engineering programmes. These demonstrate new technology and prove its effectiveness before it is incorporated in new or established designs of engine.

The modular construction of the RB211 has allowed engine performance to be uprated steadily. Technical improvements to individual engine modules have permitted operators to improve the performance of their existing engines. This technique has been applied very successfully to the RB211 engine family. As a result, many operators of RB211-powered Boeing 747s have upgraded the performance of their engines and improved the payload/range performance of their aircraft. This has been particularly valuable for flights over long ranges, such as non-stop from Hong Kong to London, where passenger loads and profitability have been greatly increased.

Advances in RB211 performance have come from improvements in high-temperature technology, materials and manufacturing techniques. For example, the life of RB211-22B high-pressure turbine blades has been transformed through using directional solidification when they are cast. As a result RB211-22B engines can now remain on the wing of aircraft they power for up to 20,000hr. Later engines have single-crystal cast turbine blades.

One of the most significant advances pioneered by Rolls-Royce is the wide-chord fan blade, introduced on the RB211-535E4 engine five years ago. Used in conjunction with a common exhaust nozzle, it gives a reduction in engine specific fuel consumption of 4-5%. Conventional solid fan blades have snubbers which act like a reinforcing ring to stabilise the blades. The snubbers restrict the airflow through the fan disc and lead to an efficiency loss where shockwaves spring from them. Rolls-Royce has developed wider and stiffer fan blades of fabricated construction which do not need snubbers. They are much more efficient aerodynamically and allow a larger airflow to pass through a given fan area. Other benefits are the wide-chord fan's excellent resistance to foreign-object damage and the quietness which it provides. Because of this, Boeing 757s with 535E4 engines can be operated at night into key US airports where 757s with Pratt & Whitney engines do not meet the noise limits.

Development of the RB211 family is continuing to increase thrust, reduce fuel consumption and enhance the commonality between engine variants. The RB211 524G/H already provides a 14% better cruise sfc (specific fuel consumption) than the initial RB211-524 engine and a further 2% improvement in cruise sfc will be achieved by late 1991 — as well as an increase in take-off thrust capability to 63,000lb. The Trent will

provide a further 2% sfc in 1993 through its increased bypass ratio and advanced intermediate-pressure compressor and low-pressure turbine. The engine benefits from features proved in other RB211 engines, as well as the Tay and V2500 turbofans. It follows the derivative design approach which has produced outstanding levels of reliability for current RB211s — including the best engine reliability in the Boeing 747 with the 524D4, according to Rolls-Royce.

A new version of the 535E4 entered service in 1989. Known as the 535E4B, it has an increased take-off thrust of 43,100lb and powers the Boeing 757s ordered by American Airlines.

Future

As indicated earlier, the RB211 family of engines has probably two-thirds of its life span still to come. It enters the 1990s with more aircraft applications than ever before and the prospect of future development to at least 80,000lb take-off thrust.

Despite its birth pangs, it has become one of the world's most successful aero engine programmes and has brought even more prestige to the famous Rolls-Royce name.

Above:
A mock-up of the new 65,000lb thrust RB211-524L engine — the Trent. Continued development will offer increased thrust up to around 80,000lb to cope with future requirements.

Below:
TWA has chosen the Trent to power its Airbus A330 airliners. The engine will also be used in the MD-11 aircraft ordered by Air Europe.